A Timeline of
Global Christianity

A Timeline of Global Christianity

One Thousand Significant Dates for Christianity across the Planet—And Beyond

BRETT KNOWLES

Foreword by Tim Cooper

RESOURCE *Publications* · Eugene, Oregon

A TIMELINE OF GLOBAL CHRISTIANITY
One Thousand Significant Dates for Christianity across the Planet—And Beyond

Copyright © 2019 Brett Knowles. All rights reserved. Except for brief quotations in critical publications or reviews, no part of this book may be reproduced in any manner without prior written permission from the publisher. Write: Permissions, Wipf and Stock Publishers, 199 W. 8th Ave., Suite 3, Eugene, OR 97401.

Encyclopedia of Christianity in the Global South, edited by Mark Lamport (2018). Used by permission of Rowman & Littlefield Publishing Group. All rights reserved.

Resource Publications
An Imprint of Wipf and Stock Publishers
199 W. 8th Ave., Suite 3
Eugene, OR 97401

www.wipfandstock.com

PAPERBACK ISBN: 978-1-5326-1822-2
HARDCOVER ISBN: 978-1-4982-4361-2
EBOOK ISBN: 978-1-4982-4360-5

Manufactured in the U.S.A.   04/20/20

To my students:
Ite, inflammate omnia
(Go forth and set the world on fire)

Attributed to Ignatius Loyola

Contents

Foreword by Tim Cooper	ix
Preface	xi
Acknowledgements	xiii
List of Abbreviations	xv
Timeline	1
Continent and Country Index	129
Name Index	135
Selected Resources	147

Foreword

It is a pleasure to speak not just for the quality of the work of scholarship you hold in your hands but also for the qualities of its author. I have known and worked with Associate Professor Knowles for fifteen years. When I first began to teach the history of Christianity here at the University of Otago, Brett was the one who pointed me towards the often-overlooked story of the Christian faith beyond the Western world. That essential steer deeply influenced the development of my own teaching. As this *Timeline of Global Christianity* makes clear, across the intervening years Brett has continued impressively to follow his own advice. This chronology is genuinely global, reinforcing one of the most dramatic and welcomed developments in the historiography over the past two decades: the recovery of non-Western Christian history. I can hardly imagine a timeline that could be more comprehensive in how it treats that history around the world and across the span of two millennia. I am confident Brett's work will prove to be of enduring service to students and their teachers, as well as the many others interested in navigating the Christian past. This work is a timely gift to us all.

Brett is an established historian in his own right. His careful scholarship and extensive knowledge will be evident in these pages. He is also an effective teacher. I know from experience just how warmly his students speak of his teaching and presence in the classroom. You can be sure Brett has undertaken the labor of compiling this timeline with the needs and capacities of students firmly in mind. Beyond all that, there is Brett as a person. I would like to place on record my regard for a colleague who has been unfailingly helpful, reliable, constructive, and

Foreword

gracious. This work is a fitting testament to his experience and stature, and I warmly commend it to you.

Tim Cooper
Associate Professor of Church History
Head of the School of Arts
University of Otago, New Zealand
August 2019

Preface

This book is written primarily as a resource for students of the History of Global Christianity. It enlarges and extends the author's twenty-seven-page timeline, previously published in the two-volume *Encyclopedia of Christianity in the Global South*,[1] and reappears by the kind permission of its publishers, Rowman and Littlefield. The timeline contains one thousand entries, covering all the inhabited continents (including the Greco-Roman World up to 565), as well as several entries relating to Christianity in Antarctica and in Outer Space. The coverage of each continent has been weighted, so that the number of entries is generally proportional to the historical span of Christianity in that continent, although the entries for Asia, Africa, Latin America and the Caribbean, and Oceania are weighted by a factor of three over those for the Greco-Roman World, Europe and North America. A small number of secular dates (e.g. 1492: Columbus's discovery of the Americas) have also been included as contextual reference points for the specifically religious events recorded in the Timeline.

The book falls into three parts. The main Timeline is arranged in date order, with a continental and country notation following each entry. These notations connect with two additional indexes, which in turn are cross-referenced back to the years listed in the Timeline. Thus the continent and country index enables the reader to follow all the events in the Timeline relating to that particular continent or country; the name index picks up the references to the most significant names appearing in the Timeline. The book can therefore be used as a simple chronological Timeline, as an index

1 . Knowles, "Timeline," 959–82.

Preface

of events occurring in each continent or country, or as a reference list of the personal names in the Timeline.

As well as being a resource for students of both secular and religious history, this book is intended as a "fire starter." The author hopes that the events recorded in its pages (both well-known and not so well-known) will ignite new sparks of historical interest for its readers and open new avenues of exploration for them. If the book fulfils these hopes, the author's purpose will have been amply accomplished.

Kia tau ki a koutou katoa te atawhai o te Ariki, o Īhu Karaiti, me te aroha o te Atua, me te whiwhinga tahitanga ki te Wairua Tapu. (May the grace of the Lord Jesus Christ, and the love of God, and the fellowship of the Holy Spirit be with you all.)

Acknowledgements

This project, like the timeline it has produced, has a history to which many people have contributed and to whom I owe my sincere thanks. The first of these is Professor Mark Lamport, who began the project's trajectory in 2016 by asking me to contribute a "Timeline of Christianity in the Global South" to the two-volume *Encyclopedia of Christianity in the Global South* that he was then preparing for publication. I also extend my thanks to Associate Professor Tim Cooper for his suggestion that the timeline be published separately as a book, and again to Professor Lamport, who enthusiastically supported this proposal. Associate Professor Cooper has also kindly contributed a foreword for the book. Finally, I offer my sincere appreciation to Rowman and Littlefield, the publishers of *Encyclopedia of Christianity in the Global South*, who graciously granted me permission to publish an extended and enlarged version of the timeline, and to Wipf and Stock, who accepted this project for publication.

I wish to acknowledge my colleagues in the Theology Programme at the University of Otago, and my Church History students, from whom I have gained much as we have explored this fascinating discipline together over the years. And last, but very definitely not least, my love and thanks to my wife Adrienne, who supported and encouraged me in the writing of this book, cheerfully enduring the chronic untidiness of my office desk (the inevitable primeval chaos that accompanies academic creation), and who made her own valuable contribution with a careful proofread of the finished text. Any errors that remain are solely the responsibility of the author.

BRETT KNOWLES
Theology Programme, University of Otago, New Zealand
November 2019

List of Abbreviations

ABCFM	American Board of Commissioners for Foreign Missions
AICs	African-Initiated Churches
ca.	circa (about, approximately)
CELAM	Consejo Episcopal Latinoamericano (Latin American Bishops' Conference)
CIA	Central Intelligence Agency
CIM	China Inland Mission
CMS	Church Missionary Society
e.g.	exempli gratia (for example)
EATWOT	Ecumenical Association of Third World Theologians
etc.	et cetera (and the rest)
fl.	floruit (flourished)
i.e.	id est (that is)
Jr.	Junior
LMS	London Missionary Society
Matt.	Gospel of Matthew
NASA	National Aeronautics and Space Administration
NGK	Nederduitse Gereformeerde Kerk (Dutch Reformed Church)

List of Abbreviations

NGS	Nederduitse Gereformeerde Sendingkirk (Dutch Reformed Mission Church, i.e. the black wing of the Dutch Reformed Church)
NZG	Nederlandsch Zendelinggenootschap (Netherlands Missionary Society)
OFM	Ordo Fratrum Minores (Little Brothers)
OP	Ordo Praedicatorium (Order of Preachers)
RENAMO	Resistência Nacional Moçambicana (Mozambique National Resistance)
SCM	Student Christian Movement
SPCK	Society for Promoting Christian Knowledge
SPG	Society for the Propagation of the Gospel in Foreign Parts
St.	Saint
SWAPO	South West Africa People's Organisation (i.e. the Namibian Independence movement)
UNSD	United Nations Statistics Division
WSCF	World Student Christian Federation

Timeline

This timeline contains one thousand entries from all six inhabited continents (and from Antarctica and Outer Space), as well as an additional category for the Greco-Roman world (which overlapped parts of the continents of Europe, Asia, and Africa up to 565). The numbers of entries for each continental category are generally proportional to the span of time covered, although entries for Asia, Africa, Latin America and the Caribbean, and Oceania are weighted by a factor of three over those for the Greco-Roman World, Europe, and North America. Europe is deemed to be that part of the Eurasian continent west of the Urals and north of the Caucasus.

The timeframes of each continental division are as follows:

- **The Greco-Roman World:** from 30 (the Crucifixion of Jesus) to 565 (the end of Justinian's reign)
- **Asia:** from 52 (the arrival of Thomas in India) up to the present
- **Africa:** from 356 (the arrival of Frumentius in Aksum) up to the present
- **Europe:** from 432 (the date of Patrick's arrival in Ireland) up to the present
- **Latin America and the Caribbean:** from 1492 (Columbus's discovery of America) up to the present
- **Oceania:** from 1521 (the entry of the first European explorers, i.e. Magellan's expedition, into the Pacific) up to the present
- **North America:** 1607 (the founding of the first colonial settlements in Virginia) up to the present

A Timeline of Global Christianity

A continental categorization follows each timeline entry, in most cases together with a reference to its modern-day equivalent location. This is derived from the United Nations Statistics Division (UNSD) website;[1] those territories not listed in the website are enclosed in rounded brackets, e.g. **(Ceuta)**, **(Taiwan)**, **(Tibet)**, etc. Entries relating to Christianity in outer space are also enclosed in rounded brackets, e.g. **(Moon: Mare Tranquillitatis)**, etc. Greenland, although included in the North American continent in the UNSD website, was historically seen as being part of Europe (i.e. a Norwegian or Danish colony) and is so treated here.

---

1. United Nations Statistics Division, "Methodology."

YEAR AND EVENT

ca.30 Forty days after the Crucifixion and Resurrection of Jesus Christ, the promised Holy Spirit fills the disciples on the Day of Pentecost and the witness of the Church begins. [**Greco-Roman World: State of Palestine**]

ca.46 The Apostle Paul begins the first of his three missionary journeys to Cyprus and Asia Minor: later journeys would take him further west into Greece, Illyricum (Albania), and, eventually, to Rome and (possibly) Spain. [**Greco-Roman World: Albania, (Cyprus), Greece, Italy, Spain, Turkey**]

49 The First Church Council meets at Jerusalem and discusses whether the requirements of the Jewish Law are binding on Gentile converts to Christianity. [**Greco-Roman World: State of Palestine**]

ca.49 Riots break out in Rome between Christians and Jews in the reign of Claudius, resulting in the expulsion of all noncitizen Jews. [**Greco-Roman World: Italy**]

50 The Apostle Paul begins writing his letters to the churches in Asia Minor, Greece, and Rome. [**Greco-Roman World: Greece, Italy, Turkey**]

52 The Apostle Thomas arrives on the Malabar Coast of southwestern India, where local Indian traditions credit him with founding seven churches (Cranganore, Quilon, Paravur, Kokkamangalam, Niranam, Palayur, and Cayal); his tomb is believed to be located at Mylapore near Chennai (Madras), on the east coast. [**Asia: India**]

62 The Sadducee Ananias (then the High Priest) brings James, the brother of Jesus and leader of the Christian community in Jerusalem, before the Sanhedrin as a lawbreaker; James is stoned to death. [**Greco-Roman World: State of Palestine**]

64 The Emperor Nero persecutes the Christians as scapegoats for the Great Fire of Rome. [**Greco-Roman World: Italy**]

ca.65–ca.95 The writing of the Gospels begins, with Mark being the first (ca.65) and John the last (ca.95) of the canonical Gospels to be composed. [**Greco-Roman World: Italy, State of Palestine, Syrian Arab Republic, Turkey**]

66–73 The First Jewish War with the Romans leads to the destruction of the Temple in Jerusalem in 70. [**Greco-Roman World: State of Palestine**]

ca.80–100 An unknown writer compiles "The Lord's Instruction (i.e. the *Didachē*) to the Gentiles through the Twelve Apostles," a compendium of recommendations on morality, community organization, and liturgy; this is possibly the earliest extant Christian writing outside the New Testament. [**Greco-Roman World: Syrian Arab Republic**]

96 Clement of Rome writes as the secretary of the church in Rome on behalf of its college of presbyters to the church of Corinth, rebuking them for the disorderly deposition of their presbyters. [**Greco-Roman World: Greece, Italy**]

104 Addai ordains Pkidha as the first Christian bishop of Arbela in Adiabene; the church there had built upon the conversion of an earlier king of Adiabene to Judaism, which (as also in the Mediterranean world) provided a beachhead for later Christian expansion. [**Asia: Iraq**]

ca.107 Ignatius of Antioch writes seven letters to the Christians in Asia and Rome while on his way to martyrdom. [**Greco-Roman World: Italy, Turkey**]

ca.112 Pliny, the Roman governor of Bithynia, writes to the Emperor Trajan seeking advice on how he should deal with those brought before his court on the charge of being Christians. [**Greco-Roman World: Turkey**]

ca.120–160 Basilides (fl. ca.120–145), a teacher in Alexandria, begins to expound Gnostic ideas, interpreting Christianity through a dualistic mindset which focusses on the acquisition of gnōsis (secret esoteric knowledge); this interpretive framework is further spread in Egypt by his disciple Valentinus (fl. ca.136–160), gaining numbers of adherents there and, after 136, in Rome also. **[Greco-Roman World: Egypt, Italy]**

ca.130–140 Aristeides of Athens and Quadratus of Asia Minor write the first Christian apologies, addressed to the Emperor Hadrian, in which they defend the Christians against the popular accusations made against them. **[Greco-Roman World: Greece, Turkey]**

132–135 Simon Bar Kochba leads a messianic Jewish revolt (also known as the Third Jewish-Roman War) in the Roman province of Judea. **[Greco-Roman World: State of Palestine]**

144 Marcion of Sinope teaches that the Jewish Yahweh is an evil Demiurge (a subordinate creator deity) and thus different from the Father of Jesus Christ; he rejects the entire Old Testament and most of the New (except for Luke's Gospel and ten of Paul's letters), on the basis that only Paul had really understood the Gospel. **[Greco-Roman World: Italy]**

ca.151 Justin Martyr addresses his *First Apology* to the Emperor Antoninus Pius, responding to pagan criticisms of Christianity and arguing that Christian theology is, in fact, the true philosophy. **[Greco-Roman World: Italy]**

156 Roman proconsular authorities in Smyrna arrest the aged Bishop Polycarp and burn him at the stake in the arena; the eyewitness account of his death becomes a paradigm for Christian martyrologies. **[Greco-Roman World: Turkey]**

ca.170 Tatian writes his Diatessarōn (lit. "through four"), the first harmony of the Gospels, in Arbela, Adiabene. **[Asia: Iraq]**

172 Montanus, together with his two disciples Maximilla and Prisca, initiates a millennial prophetic movement ("the New Prophecy") in Phrygia, claiming to speak by the direct agency of the Holy Spirit. **[Greco-Roman World: Turkey]**

177 A vicious, but short-term, persecution breaks out in Vienne and Lyons, resulting in a number of Christians being tortured and executed. **[Greco-Roman World: France]**

180 The first persecution in the province of Africa Proconsularis takes place under the proconsul Saturninus, in which twelve Christians (the "Martyrs of Scilli") are brought to trial and executed at Carthage. **[Greco-Roman World: Tunisia]**

ca.180–190 The Church of Alexandria sends its great scholar Pantaenus on a teaching mission to India. **[Asia: India; Greco-Roman World: Egypt]**

189 The Quartodeciman controversy emerges over the date of Easter, with the Asian churches keeping this on the fourteenth day of the first month of the lunar calendar (i.e. the same day as the Jewish Passover and therefore not limited to a particular day of the week) and the rest of the Church celebrating it on the Lord's Day (i.e. Easter Sunday). **[Greco-Roman World: France, Italy, Turkey]**

ca.190 Clement of Alexandria succeeds Pantaenus as the head of the catechetical school at Alexandria and lays the foundation for the integration of philosophy and Christian belief in the formulation of theology. **[Greco-Roman World: Egypt]**

ca.190 Irenaeus formulates the "Rule of Faith" as a summary of the Church's teaching, taught throughout the whole world (i.e. *kataholos*—"according to the whole," from which the word "Catholic" is derived). **[Greco-Roman World: France]**

Before 195 Following the conversion of Abgar VIII, king of Osrhoene, Edessa becomes, in the Syrian tradition, the capital of the first Christian kingdom. **[Asia: Turkey]**

196 The Syriac writer Bardaisan reports in his *Book of the Laws of Countries* that Christians are to be found as far east as the empire of the Kaishans (Bactrians) in the Hindu Kush. **[Asia: Afghanistan, Pakistan, Tajikistan, Uzbekistan]**

ca.197 Tertullian, the first important Christian writer in Latin, addresses his *Apology* to the imperial governors and magistrates, arguing that persecution of the Christians is contrary to justice and to Roman legal precedence, and demonstrating the reasonableness of Christianity. **[Greco-Roman World: Tunisia]**

201 The city records of Edessa (the *Chronicle of Edessa*) note the destruction of the first recorded church building ("the church of the Christians") by a major flood. **[Asia: Turkey]**

203 The Roman authorities arrest several Christians, including Perpetua and Felicitas, but fail to persuade them to sacrifice to the Emperor; these women are martyred by being exposed to wild beasts in the arena at Carthage. [**Greco-Roman World: Tunisia**]

207 Tertullian leaves the Catholic Church and joins the Montanists; this indicates that the latter are broadly doctrinally orthodox, despite their opponents' accusations to the contrary. [**Greco-Roman World: Tunisia**]

ca.215 The *Apostolic Tradition*, attributed to Hippolytus of Rome, sets out an array of liturgical standards for the discipling of catechumens (persons receiving instruction in the Christian faith) and the conduct of public liturgy. [**Greco-Roman World: Italy**]

ca.220–230 Origen writes his *De Principiis* (*On First Principles*), the first Christian systematic theology. [**Greco-Roman World: Egypt**]

225 The sixth-century Syriac *Chronicle of Arbela*, written by Mĕšīḥā-Zĕḵā, records that there are more than twenty bishops in Mesopotamia and the Persian Gulf by this date. [**Asia: Iraq, Islamic Republic of Iran (Persia), Qaṭar; Greco-Roman World: Syrian Arab Republic**]

231 The Church of Caesarea ordains Origen as a presbyter, but this ordination is held to be invalid because he had made himself a eunuch (on the basis of his literal interpretation of Matt.19:12); consequently he is excommunicated by his home church of Alexandria. [**Greco-Roman World: Egypt, State of Palestine**]

250–251 The Emperor Decius launches the first official, Empire-wide persecution of the Christians (previous persecutions had been sporadic outbreaks of local mob violence, rather than the product of Imperial policy); records of this persecution come from Rome, Jerusalem, Antioch, and Carthage. [**Greco-Roman World: Italy, State of Palestine, Tunisia, Turkey**]

251 Cyprian, bishop of Carthage, writes his *De Unitate Catholicae Ecclesiae* (*On the Unity of the Catholic Church*), insisting that schism violates the essential nature of the church, the unity of which is focused in its bishops; this episcopal network guarantees the cohesion of the whole diverse body. [**Greco-Roman World: Tunisia**]

A Timeline of Global Christianity

251 The Novatianist schism breaks out in Rome over the readmission to communion of lapsed Christians who had apostatized or denied the faith during persecution. [**Greco-Roman World: Italy**]

258 Although he had fled in order to lead his church from hiding during the Decian persecution (249–251), Cyprian of Carthage is arrested and martyred in the later persecution under Valerian. [**Greco-Roman World: Tunisia**]

268 A synod of bishops deposes Paul of Samosata, the bishop of Antioch, for his teaching that Jesus is essentially a uniquely inspired man, rather than the preexistent divine Son of God by nature. [**Greco-Roman World: Turkey**]

ca.270 Antony of Egypt goes into the desert as an ascetic hermit, laying the foundations for the monastic movement; this solitary asceticism develops into an organized community by 305. [**Greco-Roman World: Egypt**]

288 Gregory "the Illuminator" returns from exile in Cappadocia to his homeland of Armenia as a missionary, but is imprisoned in a pit by King Tiridates III for thirteen years; eventually the king is converted and Christianity becomes the official faith of Armenia in 301. [**Asia: Armenia**]

303–311 Diocletian and his co-Emperors launch a series of edicts against the Christians in an attempt to preserve the stability of the Roman Empire and to revitalize its pagan religious life; these final Empire-wide persecutions together would become known as "the Great Persecution." [**Greco-Roman World**]

311 Galerius (the co-Emperor with Constantine) issues an Edict of Toleration, ending the persecution of Christians in the Roman Empire. [**Greco-Roman World**]

311–312 The election of Bishop Caecilian of Carthage leads to the rise of the Donatists as a "church of the pure," who had maintained a steadfast testimony in persecution, in contrast to those African Catholics who had handed over their copies of the Scriptures to be burned. [**Greco-Roman World: Algeria, Tunisia**]

312 The conversion of the Emperor Constantine, through his vision of a cross of light at the Battle of the Milvian Bridge, leads to his issuing (together with his co-Emperor Licinius) of the Edict of Milan the following year granting full toleration to all religions (including the Christians) in the Roman Empire. [**Greco-Roman World: Italy**]

318 Arius, a presbyter of the church of Alexandria, takes issue with a sermon by its bishop Alexander, and questions whether the Son could be said to be God in the same way that the Father was; this local dispute escalates into the Empire-wide Arian controversy by 324. [**Greco-Roman World: Egypt**]

320s Pachomius founds a new type of community in the Thēbaïd desert in Southern Egypt, patterned on coenobitic monasticism (the Christian life lived in community, rather than in ascetic isolation). [**Greco-Roman World: Egypt**]

321 Constantine makes Sunday, the Christian day of rest, obligatory for all citizens (whether Christian or pagan) throughout the Roman Empire. [**Greco-Roman World**]

325 Eusebius of Caesarea publishes his *Ecclesiastical History*, the first church history, which climaxes with the conversion and reign of Constantine as virtually the fulfillment of the Kingdom of God upon Earth. [**Greco-Roman World: State of Palestine**]

325 The Council of Nicaea condemns Arianism and issues the Nicene Creed as a statement of orthodox Christian belief. [**Greco-Roman World: Turkey**]

328 Athanasius, the steadfast defender of the Creed of Nicaea against its Arian opponents, becomes bishop of Alexandria. [**Greco-Roman World: Egypt**]

330 The Emperor Constantine transfers the capital of the Roman Empire from Rome to Constantinople. [**Greco-Roman World: Italy, Turkey**]

ca.330 Christianity arrives in Georgia through the witness of a Christian Cappadocian slave girl (Nino), whose healing powers cure the ailing Georgian Queen Nana. [**Asia: Georgia**]

337 Just before his death, Constantine finally receives baptism as a catechumen (a person receiving instruction in the Christian faith). [**Greco-Roman World: Turkey**]

337–361 Secular and religious strife follows Constantine's death, with his three sons (Constans, Constantius II, and Constantine II) taking opposing sides in the Arian controversy, leading to civil war in the Empire. [**Greco-Roman World**]

340–363 The Great Persecution of the Persian church begins under King Šāpur II, lasting until the accession of Julian "the Apostate" as Emperor of the Roman Empire (when the Persian Christians could no longer be accused of being allies of a Christian Roman Emperor); after some years of peace, the persecution is reignited sporadically from ca.379 until ca.401. [**Asia: Iraq, Islamic Republic of Iran (Persia)**]

341 Ulfilas begins missionary work among the barbarian Goths, converting them to Arian Christianity. [**Europe: Germany**]

345 Nestorian merchant Thomas Kināyi, accompanied by a party of four hundred Persian Christians possibly fleeing persecution in Persia, arrives in Cranganore on the Malabar Coast to settle. [**Asia: India**]

Before 356 Following his shipwreck in the Red Sea while returning from a missionary journey to India with his guardian, Frumentius becomes an official in the Aksumite court of King Ella Amida, where he converts members of the king's household; after going back to Egypt some years later he is consecrated in Alexandria and returns to Ethiopia as bishop of Aksum. [**Africa: Eritrea, Ethiopia**]

356 A Roman Mission to India under the Arian Theophilus the Deacon (also known as "Theophilus the Indian," since he is a native of the Maldives Islands, southwest of Kerala) visits Southwest Arabia, converting its Ḥimyarite ruler and building short-lived churches at Aden, Ẓafār, Sanʿāʾ, and Hormuz; more enduring results follow from the activity of the Nestorian Arab convert Ḥayyān fifty years later (399–420). [**Asia: Yemen**]

357 A small gathering of bishops, the Council of Sirmium, issues a doctrinal statement that came to be known as "the Blasphemy of Sirmium" for its defective definition of the Trinity. [**Greco-Roman World: Serbia**]

360s–370s Basil of Caesarea, his younger brother Gregory of Nyssa, and his friend Gregory of Nazianzus (collectively known as the "Three Cappadocians" or the "Cappadocian Fathers") help to define Christology in terms of modes of being rather than of substance, leading to the final repudiation of Arianism and the reaffirmation of the Nicene faith at the Council of Constantinople in 381. [**Greco-Roman World: Turkey**]

361–363 A pagan reaction to the Christian conflict over doctrine takes place under Julian the Apostate (so called because he had been brought up as a Christian but had renounced his faith on his elevation to the Imperial throne). [**Greco-Roman World: Turkey**]

366–384 Bishop Damasus of Rome consolidates the authority of the Roman church, emphasizing its apostolic founding by Peter and promoting the primacy of its bishop, leading to the development of the papacy. [**Greco-Roman World: Italy**]

367 Athanasius sets out the canonical books of the New Testament, the first such list that exactly matches our current canon. [**Greco-Roman World: Egypt**]

370s Monasticism begins to shift from the deserts to the towns under the influence of Basil of Caesarea, leading to a focus on communal living, rather than on isolation and asceticism. [**Greco-Roman World: State of Palestine**]

373 Māwiyya, the first Christian Arab queen, becomes leader of the western Tanakh in the Syrian/Arabian desert on the death of her husband, the tribal sheikh; the tribe had been converted through the influence of miracle-working priests and monks about ten years earlier. [**Asia: Saudi Arabia, Syrian Arab Republic**]

378–383 Jerome begins the translation of the Bible into Latin, firstly in Rome and later in Bethlehem; this translation would become known as the Vulgate (Latin: *vulgata*, or "common") version. [**Greco-Roman World: State of Palestine**]

379 Christianity becomes the state religion of the Roman Empire under Theodosius I. [**Greco-Roman World: Turkey**]

381 The first Council of Constantinople further refines the Nicene definition of Christology. [**Greco-Roman World: Turkey**]

385 Augustine of Hippo abandons Manichaeism (a dualistic religion which saw the world as a cosmic warfare between the eternal principles of light and darkness, both conceived in material terms), although elements of this might have continued to influence his views on the transmission of Original Sin. [**Greco-Roman World: Tunisia**]

A Timeline of Global Christianity

386 Augustine of Hippo converts to Catholic Christianity through the influence of Bishop Ambrose of Milan; as he records it in his *Confessions*, the key catalyst is a child playing in the next-door garden, calling *"Tolle, lege!"* ("Take, read!" i.e. the Bible). [**Greco-Roman World: Italy**]

387 Public responses to the Emperor Theodosius's arrest and execution of the participants in riots in Antioch (in which the statues of the imperial family had been defaced) demonstrate the growing power of the Christian pulpit in the fourth century. [**Greco-Roman World: Turkey**]

390 Bishop Ambrose of Milan refuses to celebrate the Eucharist in the presence of the Emperor Theodosius (effectively an act of excommunication) because of his responsibility for the massacre of seven thousand people at Thessalonika, forcing Theodosius to do public penance before being restored to communion. [**Greco-Roman World: Greece, Italy**]

395 Augustine becomes a coadjutor bishop at Hippo and sole bishop the following year. [**Greco-Roman World: Tunisia**]

5th and 6th centuries Christianity becomes widespread on the pre-Islamic Arabian Peninsula; examples of this include the Christian kingdoms of the Lakhmids (Northern Arabia/Iraq) and Kinda (central Arabia), the flourishing dioceses of Bahrain, Qaṭar, and Oman, and the martyr bishops of Yemen. [**Asia: Bahrain, Iraq, Oman, Qaṭar, Saudi Arabia, Yemen**]

404 Bishop John Chrysostom's blunt, tactless exhortations to moral reformation make him widely unpopular (especially in the Imperial Court) and lead to his banishment from Constantinople to exile in Armenia. [**Greco Roman World: Turkey**]

410 Following an Edict of Toleration issued the previous year by Shah Yazdegerd I, the Persian Church organizes itself as a separate, distinct, and autonomous church at the "Synod of Isaac," held at Seleucia-Ctesiphon, and declares the Catholicos (Primate) of Seleucia-Ctesiphon to be supreme among the churches of the East. [**Asia: Iraq, Islamic Republic of Iran (Persia)**]

410 The City of Rome falls to the Goths and other barbarian invaders, marking the symbolic end of the Roman Empire in the West. [**Greco-Roman World: Italy**]

410 Twenty years after the Persian Nestorian missionary 'Abdisho had established a monastery in Bahrain, delegates from Bahrain and Qatar attend the Nestorian "Synod of Isaac" at Seleucia-Ctesiphon. [**Asia: Bahrain, Qatar**]

412 Cyril becomes the bishop of Alexandria and begins to ruthlessly suppress dissent (e.g. his nonintervention in the murder of the Neoplatonist teacher Hypatia by a mob in 415 and his attacks on Nestorius, whose condemnation by the Council of Ephesus in 431 is largely due to Cyril's machinations). [**Greco-Roman World: Egypt, Turkey**]

418 The Council of Carthage condemns Pelagianism (an emphasis on the role of human works in the obtaining of salvation). [**Greco-Roman World: Tunisia**]

424 The Synod of Dādīšo' (Dadyeshu) at Markabta asserts the independent authority of the Catholicos of Seleucia-Ctesiphon from, and his equal rank with, any western Patriarch. [**Asia: Iraq, Islamic Republic of Iran (Persia)**]

431 The Council of Ephesus excommunicates Nestorius because of his imputed teaching on the two *distinct* natures (Divine and human) of Christ. [**Greco-Roman World: Turkey**]

432 Patrick arrives in Ireland about this date and converts King Lóegaire mac Néill (Laoghaire), the High King of Ireland, at Tara. [**Europe: Ireland**]

440 Pope Leo I assumes a number of civic, as well as religious, responsibilities due to the collapse of the Roman government in the western Empire after the Fall of Rome. [**Greco-Roman World: Italy**]

449 The "Robber Council" (Latin: *latrocinium*, "den of robbers") meets in Ephesus; Dioscorus, bishop of Alexandria, presides and by means of violence, intimidation, and corruption achieves his goals of reversing the decisions of earlier councils and of deposing his opponents from their sees. [**Greco-Roman World: Turkey**]

451 The Council of Chalcedon consolidates the edicts of previous councils and issues the classic orthodox definition of the Divine and human natures of Christ *united* in the one person (sometimes referred to as Dyophysite, or "two natures" theology). [**Greco-Roman World: Turkey**]

A Timeline of Global Christianity

452 Pope Leo I makes an embassy to Attila the Hun, the leader of a devastating barbarian invasion into Europe, seeking to alleviate the effects of this offensive and to dissuade the barbarians from sacking Rome. [**Greco-Roman World: Italy**]

452–457 A theological revolt in Egypt in 452 leads to the establishment of Coptic (i.e. Monophysite/Miaphysite, "one nature") churches in Egypt and Ethiopia; five years later, the Chalcedonian Dyophysite Patriarch of Alexandria is killed in a street riot. [**Africa: Egypt**]

Before 480 A group of Dyophysite Syrian monks known as the "Nine Saints" arrives in Aksum, where they convert its inhabitants, set up monasteries, and translate the Bible into Geʿez. [**Africa: Eritrea, Ethiopia**]

486 The Synod of Mār ʿAqaq (Acacius) moves the Persian Church away from both Chalcedonian orthodoxy and Monophysitism and toward a Nestorian definition of the Trinity. [**Asia: Iraq, Islamic Republic of Iran (Persia)**]

489 The metropolitan archbishop Bar Ṣaumā founds a Nestorian school at Nisibis (then in Persian territory), which becomes the key institution in the revitalization and Nestorianizing of the Persian Church in the sixth century. [**Asia: Turkey**]

496 Chlodovocar (Clovis), the King of the Franks, adopts Catholic Christianity (the first barbarian king to do so) and is baptized. [**Europe: Belgium, France, Netherlands**]

497–498 Following a coup d'état in Persia, the Sassanian king Kavad takes refuge with the White Huns, creating links that would lead to their later evangelization and contribute to the expansion of Christianity in Central Asia. [**Asia: Afghanistan, China, India, Kazakhstan, Kyrgyzstan, Pakistan, Tajikistan, Turkmenistan, Uzbekistan**]

520 Kaleb, the king of Aksum, invades Yemen, where the Ḥimyarite king Dhū Nuwās is persecuting Christians, both in Yemen and (especially) at Najrān, the key Christian center in Southern Arabia; Kaleb defeats him and appoints the native Christian Sumuafaʾ Ashawaʾ as viceroy, leading to Southern Arabia becoming a Christian territory under Ethiopian hegemony for the next fifty years. [**Africa: Eritrea, Ethiopia; Asia: Yemen**]

527–565 The Emperor Justinian seeks to restore the Roman Empire in the West, abolish the last remnants of paganism, and strengthen the Orthodox Church; he achieves these aims by building splendid churches such as the Hagia Sophia (Holy Wisdom), by codifying its liturgy, and by consolidating Roman law on a Christian basis (the Code of Justinian). [**Greco-Roman World: Algeria, Bosnia and Herzegovina, Croatia, Italy, Libya, Morocco, Slovenia, Spain, Tunisia**]

529 Benedict of Nursia founds the Abbey of Monte Cassino, which becomes a paradigm for Benedictine monasteries for more than fourteen hundred years until it is destroyed in 1943 during the Second World War. [**Europe: Italy**]

ca.530 Benedict of Nursia writes his Rule, setting out the classic standard of monastic community life; this became the dominant pattern of monasticism in Europe throughout the Middle Ages. [**Europe: Italy**]

540 Mār Aḇā becomes the Patriarch of the East and introduces reforms in the Persian church, reorganizing its discipline, reinvigorating its theological education, reviving its spiritual and moral tone, and attempting to bring unity. [**Asia: Iraq, Islamic Republic of Iran (Persia)**]

ca.542–578 Monophysite (i.e. Jacobite Syrian Orthodox) churches expand from Syria to India, largely through the journeys of Jacob al-Barād'i. [**Asia: India, Iraq, Islamic Republic of Iran (Persia)**]

543 The Monophysite monk Julian (sent by the Byzantine Empress Theodora) arrives in the kingdom of Nobatia, where he converts the royal court to Monophysitism and facilitates Christianity's spread throughout the kingdom. [**Africa: Sudan**]

551 Two Nestorian monks arrive in the Court of Justinian, bringing silkworms, probably from the petty Turkic kingdoms to the west of China, rather than from China itself. [**Asia: (Turkestan: Central Asia)**]

555 The Nestorian merchant and explorer Cosmas Indicopleustes encounters Christians in Socotra during his voyage to Taprobane (Sri Lanka) and Kerala (South India). [**Asia: India, Sri Lanka, Yemen**]

563 Columba and his followers cross the Irish Sea to Scotland, then comprising part of the Ulster Gaelic kingdom of Dalriada, on *peregrinatio* (i.e. wandering: the characteristic Celtic monastic practice of following Christ by means of pilgrimage or voluntary exile) and found a monastery on the island of Hii (Iona) off the west coast of Scotland.

[Europe: United Kingdom of Great Britain and Northern Ireland (Scotland)]

569 Makouria, the central and smallest African Nubian kingdom, converts from Monophysitism to Chalcedonian Christianity. [**Africa: Sudan**]

569–571 A Persian monastic revival begins under Abraham of Kaskar (the founder of the Mount Izla monastery) and the monastery's abbot Mār Bābay; this is typified by education, mobility, and outreach, extending as far as China by 635. [**Asia: Iraq, Islamic Republic of Iran (Persia)**]

578 The Nestorian family of Mār Sargis emigrates to Lin-T'ao in the province of Kansu, becoming possibly the first Nestorians to settle in China. [**Asia: China**]

580 The Egyptian Bishop of Philae converts Alwa/Alodia, the southernmost Nubian kingdom, to Monophysite Christianity. [**Africa: Sudan**]

590 Pope Gregory I ("the Great") begins his reign and dispatches papal missions to Gaul, Sardinia, and (especially) England, with Augustine of Canterbury arriving in Kent in 596. [**Europe: France, Italy, United Kingdom of Great Britain and Northern Ireland (England)**]

ca.590 The Celtic monk Columbanus leaves Ireland to begin missionary work in Burgundy; he later bases his evangelistic work near Lake Constance in Switzerland and at Bobbio in Italy. [**Europe: France, Germany, Ireland, Italy**]

591 Numbers of captured Turkish prisoners, fighting in Central Asia as Persian allies, arrive in Constantinople and are found to have crosses tattooed on their foreheads to ward off pestilence. [**Asia: (Turkestan: Central Asia)**]

597 The papal mission to England achieves dramatic early success, with King Ethelbert of Kent and thousands of his subjects being baptized in the Thames on Christmas Day 597; Canterbury (Kent City) becomes the headquarters of the new English church and Augustine of Canterbury its first archbishop. [**Europe: United Kingdom of Great Britain and Northern Ireland (England)**]

610 Muḥammad begins to receive revelations in a cave outside Mecca and is commanded to recite these (Iqra' i.e. "Recite!" from which the word Qur'ān, i.e. "what is recited," is derived). [**Asia: Saudi Arabia**]

622 Muḥammad flees from Mecca to Medina; this escape is known as the Hijrah or Hejira ("emigration" or "journey"), marking the first year in the Muslim calendar. [**Asia: Saudi Arabia**]

Early 630s Emissaries from a number of petty states in the Tarim Basin (modern-day Xinjiang Uyghur Autonomous Region) arrive in the T'ang Imperial Court, reflecting increased Chinese contact with, and openness to, the West. [**Asia: China, (Turkestan: Central Asia)**]

635 Alopen and a number of Nestorian monks arrive at the T'ang Imperial Court in Ch'ang-An (Xian-fu); their arrival marks the beginning of a Christian presence in China. [**Asia: China**]

638 Arab Muslim armies under 'Umar I conquer Jerusalem; 'Umar declines an invitation from the Christian bishop to pray in the Church of the Holy Sepulchre (since this would furnish the precedent for a claim on the part of zealous Muslims to the church as a mosque), thus preserving it as a Christian house of worship. [**Asia: State of Palestine**]

638 The T'ang Emperor Tai-Tsung issues an Edict of Universal Toleration for foreign religions (including Christians) in China and orders the building of a monastery for twenty-one Nestorian monks in Ch'ang-An under Imperial patronage. [**Asia: China**]

640–670 The Arab takeover of Egypt and North Africa extends along the Mediterranean coast to Tunis; but further south, two attacks on Northern Nubia are driven back by Nubian archers (known as the "pupil-piercers" because of their accuracy), leading to a *baqt* (pact) recognizing Nubia's independence. [**Africa: Egypt, Libya, Sudan**]

657 A letter from the Catholicos Isho'yabh III to the Metropolitan Shem'on refers to a Nestorian Episcopate of India, extending from the borders of Persia to "Qlh" (possibly Klang, on the west coast of the Malay Peninsula). [**Asia: Malaysia**]

664 King Oswy chooses Roman Christianity over Celtic Christianity at the Synod of Whitby in Northumbria; the merger of these two churches has significant implications for missions to continental Europe, which thereafter combine the Celts' charismatic passion with the Romans' talent for organization and consolidation. [**Europe: United Kingdom of Great Britain and Northern Ireland (England)**]

665–689 The Arabs extend their conquests of North Africa from Tunis to Morocco, thus bringing all of coastal North Africa under Muslim control. [**Africa: Algeria, Morocco, Tunisia**]

687 Pepin of Heristal unites the Franks into a cohesive kingdom, thus laying the foundation for the later partnership between the Frankish kings and the Catholic Church. [**Europe: Austria, Belgium, France, Germany, Liechtenstein, Luxembourg, Netherlands, Switzerland**]

690 Willibrord evangelizes the Franks in Belgium and Holland, becoming their bishop in 695. [**Europe: Belgium, Netherlands**]

698 Persecution of the Christians in China begins under the ruthless and fanatically pro-Buddhist Empress Wu Hou (who been the concubine of the previous Emperor Kao-Tsung, and had usurped the throne from her late husband and two sons). [**Asia: China**]

By 701 Makouria annexes its northern neighbor Nobatia, with the enlarged state adhering to Monophysite Christianity. [**Africa: Sudan**]

711–716 The Arab armies enter Spain, defeating the Christian Visigoths and establishing al-Andalus, a province of the Umayyad Caliphate, at Cordoba in Southern Spain. [**Europe: Spain**]

716 Boniface (Wynfrith) makes his first missionary journey to Frisia; six years later, he is consecrated in Rome as bishop-without-see for the German frontier regions, giving him plenipotentiary authority over the church there. [**Europe: Germany, Italy, Netherlands**]

731 The Venerable Bede completes his *Ecclesiastical History of the English People*; his text provides much of the data for later understandings of early English Christianity. [**Europe: United Kingdom of Great Britain and Northern Ireland (England)**]

732 Charles Martel and the Franks halt the Arab advance into Europe at the Battle of Poitiers. [**Europe: France**]

735 A Persian (and possibly Nestorian) physician accompanies the Chinese official Dōsen (Dao Xuan) on an embassy to Japan from the T'ang Chinese Court; this physician, who is given an official court rank and the Japanese name of Rimitsu, may therefore represent the first Christian contact with Japan, although no continuing Christian community results from his visit. [**Asia: Japan**]

739 The inscriptions of the monk Theophilus on the walls of his cave dwelling near Faras include the famous Rotas-Sator palindrome, indicating Nubia's ongoing links with the wider Christian world. [**Africa: Sudan**]

750 The 'Abbasid dynasty replaces that of the Umayyads at Baghdād; this more Asian and more strictly orthodox new dynasty places greater importance on religious, rather than racial, identity, and gradually introduces greater restrictions on Christians; however, it also begins the translation of Greek texts into Syriac and thence into Arabic, leading to the development of Islamic philosophical, medical, and scientific learning. [**Asia: Iraq**]

751 Pepin, the son of Charles Martel and grandson of Pepin of Heristal, deposes the Merovingian king Childeric and begins the Carolingian dynasty as Pepin III, inaugurating a codependent partnership between the Frankish kings and the papacy; his son Charlemagne becomes its most powerful king in 771. [**Europe: Austria, Belgium, France, Germany, Liechtenstein, Luxembourg, Netherlands, Switzerland**]

751 The 'Abbasid Caliphate's victory over the T'ang Chinese army at the Talas River in the Pamirs represents a high-tide mark of Arab expansion in Central Asia (leading to the region's permanent conversion to Islam); it also marks the end of T'ang hegemony west of the Pamirs, and the beginnings of five centuries of Chinese military decline. [**Asia: Kyrgyzstan**]

754 A band of pagan Frisians ambush and martyr the English Roman missionary Boniface, along with fifty-two companions, as he is reading the Scriptures to his neophyte Christian converts in preparation for their confirmation on Pentecost Sunday. [**Europe: Netherlands**]

779 Benedict of Aniane founds a monastery that becomes a center of Benedictine reform for all French monastic houses; his Rule of Benedict (not to be confused with the earlier Rule of Benedict of Nursia) is approved as a monastic standard at the Council of Aachen in 817. [**Europe: France**]

779 The Catholicos Timotheos I, a native of Adiabene and the greatest of the Nestorian patriarchs, rules the Church of the East from 779 to

823 from his seat in Baghdād, the new capital, where he is active in the 'Abbasid court. [**Asia: Iraq**]

781 The Catholicos Timotheos I appoints a bishop for Tibet and engages in a public debate with the Caliph Mahdī on Islam and Christianity, making that year a highpoint for Nestorian Christianity in the Islamic world. [**Asia: Iraq, (Tibet)**]

781 The Nestorian chorepiscopus (rural bishop) Mār Yazdbozid (Issu) erects a monument in Xi'an-fu, inscribed by his son, the monk-bishop and scholar Ching-Ching (Adam), commemorating the arrival of Christianity in China; this monument is rediscovered in 1623. [**Asia: China**]

781 The scholar Alcuin of York becomes an advisor to Charlemagne, joining an influential group of scholars at the royal court and thereby helping to launch the "Carolingian Renaissance." [**Europe: Germany**]

800 The coronation of Charlemagne as Holy Roman Emperor during a Christmas Day mass at St. Peter's Basilica in Rome installs him as the heir to the Caesars and thus the legitimate ruler of Europe, thereby distancing the Roman church from Byzantine rule. [**Europe: Italy**]

814 Louis the Pious succeeds his father Charlemagne as Holy Roman Emperor; on his death in 840, the Carolingian Empire disintegrates into three fragmentary kingdoms, collapsing in the late ninth century following further barbarian invasions by the Hungarians, the Vikings, and the Moslems. [**Europe: Austria, Belgium, Czechia (Czech Republic), France, Germany, Italy, Liechtenstein, Luxembourg, Netherlands, Poland, Slovakia, Slovenia, Spain, Switzerland**]

829 After an unsuccessful attempt to evangelize Denmark (826–828) under the patronage of its king Harald Klak, Anskar goes to Sweden in response to a request from the Swedish king Björg for a missionary and organizes a small congregation at Birka, on Lake Mälaren. [**Europe: Denmark, Sweden**]

836 King Georgios I of Makouria visits Baghdād and reaffirms the *baqt* of ca.650 with the 'Abbasid Caliphate; under his rule Makouria becomes powerful, with a strong alliance between the Nubian church and the Nubian state. [**Africa: Sudan**]

840–846 A vicious xenophobic persecution breaks out under the Emperor Wu-tsung, with all foreign religions (Manichaeanism, Zoroastrianism,

Nestorian Christianity, and, especially, Buddhism) being banned and/or expelled from China in 846. [**Asia: China**]

851 Five years after the expulsion of the Christians from China, Ibn Wahb, an Arab visitor to the Chinese Imperial Court, notes the Emperor Xuan-tsung's familiarity with Biblical stories (e.g. Noah, Moses, and Jesus), during an audience with him.[2] [**Asia: China**]

851 The Norwegian Viking chieftain Olaf the White sets up a pagan kingdom in Dublin; this would last for the next three centuries. [**Europe: Ireland**]

857 Anskar becomes archbishop of Hamburg and as such, the Metropolitan of all the northern (i.e. Germanic) churches. [**Europe: Germany**]

863 Two brothers, Cyril and Methodius, begin Orthodox missions among the Slavs in Moravia at the request of Ratislav, the Slavic ruler and prince of Moravia. [**Europe: Czechia (Czech Republic)**]

864 A delegation from Constantinople baptizes Boris I, king of Bulgaria; six years later Boris persuades the Emperor and the Ecumenical Patriarch of Constantinople to approve an independent Bulgarian church organization, subject to the Ecumenical Patriarch and conducting its liturgy in the Slavonic language. [**Europe: Bulgaria**]

867 Pope Adrian II approves the Slavonic liturgy of Cyril and Methodius. [**Europe: Italy**]

870 Parties of Viking Norsemen arrive in Iceland and find communities of Irish Catholics already established there. [**Europe: Iceland**]

871–899 Alfred the Great defeats the Danish invaders of Wessex, forcing their conversion to Christianity; he later promotes the recovery of Christian learning by the appointment of pious, educated, and trustworthy bishops and abbots, and by the establishment of a court school. [**Europe: United Kingdom of Great Britain and Northern Ireland (England)**]

878 As the T'ang dynasty weakens in the last quarter of the ninth century, rebellions against the throne increase and imperial protection of foreign religions declines; in one of these rebellions, a massacre of one hundred twenty thousand foreigners, including Christians, takes place in the port city of Guangzhou (Canton). [**Asia: China**]

---

2. al-Sīrāfī, "Akhbār al-Ṣīn w'al-Hind," 54–55.

907 The abdication of the fourteen-year-old Emperor Ai ends the T'ang Dynasty in China. [**Asia: China**]

910 The establishment of the Abbey of Cluny in Burgundy brings about a series of changes in medieval monasticism and fosters a renewal of monastic spirituality within the Western Church, based on its model of monastic independence from the local aristocracy and episcopacy. [**Europe: France**]

911 A treaty signed at St. Clair-sur-Epte between King Charles the Simple of France and the Viking chieftain Rollo grants the Vikings territory in northwestern France (the Duchy of Normandy); these Viking settlers became known as "Normans" (Norsemen or "North-men"). [**Europe: France**]

948 Adam of Bremen records the appointment of the first Danish bishops (under the authority of the archbishop of Hamburg) in the province of Jutland during the reign of Harald Bluetooth (Harald I). [**Europe: Denmark**]

955 The Germanic emperor Otto I defeats the Magyars near Augsburg, bringing about the end of the eastern Barbarian invasions until the time of Mongols in the thirteenth century; the Magyars settle in Hungary, which thus becomes a "buffer state" between the Germanic kingdoms and the Asian barbarians. [**Europe: Germany, Hungary**]

957 The Kievan Grand Princess Olga visits Constantinople, where she is baptized into the Orthodox Church. [**Europe: Belarus, Russian Federation, Ukraine**]

962 The coronation of Otto as Charlemagne's successor, one and a half centuries after the end of the Carolingian era, marks the restoration of the "Holy Roman Empire"; this multiethnic association of territories in Western and Central Europe would continue until its dissolution in 1806. [**Europe: Germany**]

966 The baptism of Polish Prince Mieszko I on his marriage to a Catholic Czech princess leads to the conversion of Poland. [**Europe: Poland**]

969–1171 The Isma'ili Shi'a Fatimid Caliphate conquers Egypt, eventually extending their territory from the Red Sea to the Atlantic Ocean; it adopts a largely tolerant attitude toward Christians and Jews. [**Africa: Egypt**]

975 Although there is some mission influence in Hungary after the end of the Magyar invasion in 955, little progress is made until the baptism of Géza (Geisa), prince of Hungary, after his marriage to the Christian princess Adelheid of Poland; as a Christian king, he seeks (whether by persuasion or by force) to turn Hungary into a Christian country, and the number of converts multiplies rapidly. [**Europe: Hungary**]

987 The 'Abbasid "Court Companion" Abu'l-Faraj records the report of a Nestorian monk sent to China seven years earlier to make contact with the remnants of the Nestorian mission, finding only one Christian remaining there; however, it appears from the monk's reference to "the perils of the sea" that he had travelled by the maritime route, and is therefore primarily referring to Southern China, rather than the whole country. [**Asia: China**]

988 The baptism of the Grand Prince Vladimir of Kiev by Byzantine missionaries leads to the conversion of Kievan Rus' to Orthodox Christianity. [**Europe: Belarus, Russian Federation, Ukraine**]

ca.990 Odinkar Hvite the Elder becomes the first bishop of Skara, the oldest bishopric in Sweden. [**Europe: Sweden**]

ca.990 Olaf Tryggvessön, later to become king of Norway, encounters (and is deeply impressed by) a Christian hermit in the Scilly Islands, and receives baptism from him. [**Europe: United Kingdom of Great Britain and Northern Ireland (Scilly Islands)**]

995 The newly crowned king of Norway, Olaf Tryggvessön, attempts to impose Christianity on his realm, dispatching missionaries to the Shetland, Faroe, and Orkney Islands, as well as to the Norse colonies of Iceland and Greenland. [**Europe: Faroe Islands, Greenland, Iceland, Norway, United Kingdom of Great Britain and Northern Ireland (Scotland)**]

ca.1000 Indian Christianity may possibly have arrived in Myanmar about this date through the influence of the Sri Lankan saga Mahavamsa. [**Asia: Myanmar (Burma)**]

1004 Following the missionary activity of the Norwegian king Olaf Tryggvessön, the Icelandic Althing (parliamentary gathering) debates Christianity and the Icelanders go over to Christianity. [**Europe: Iceland**]

A Timeline of Global Christianity

1009 Ebedyeshu, the Nestorian Metropolitan of Merv, reports that a Kerait prince had requested baptism from the Nestorians and that the prince and two hundred thousand of his subjects had been baptized. **[Asia: Mongolia]**

1009–1016 Abu 'Ali al-Ḥākim bi-'Amr-Allāh (the "mad Caliph") persecutes the Coptic Church in Egypt, later executing Christian officials and ordering the destruction of Church of the Holy Sepulchre in Jerusalem. **[Africa: Egypt; Asia: State of Palestine, Syrian Arab Republic]**

1016 Following the adoption of Christianity by the Althing in 1004, the Icelandic church takes institutional form with the establishment of the first two bishoprics (Skálholt and Hólar). **[Europe: Iceland]**

1016 Olaf Haraldssön becomes king of Norway and, building on the previous gains of Olaf Tryggvessön, seeks to make Christianity permanent in his realm. **[Europe: Norway]**

1022 The Danish king Knut sends his Danish bishops to the Archbishop of Canterbury for consecration, rather than to Hamburg (the metropolitan see for all of the northern nations), reflecting the increase of English missions in Scandinavia and the decline of Germanic influence. **[Europe: Denmark]**

1026 King Knut undertakes a pilgrimage to Rome, thus symbolically linking the Germanic and Roman worlds. **[Europe: Denmark]**

1046 The Holy Roman Emperor Henry III deposes three rival popes and inaugurates a papal reform movement. **[Europe: Germany]**

1049 Leo IX becomes pope and begins church reform by seeking to abolish "simony" (i.e. the appointment of church officials by local lords and princes). **[Europe: Italy]**

1054 The Great Schism between the Eastern and Western Churches worsens, with the papal Legate Humbert of Silva Candida and the Orthodox Patriarch Michael Cerularius anathematizing each other in Constantinople. **[Asia: Turkey; Europe: Italy]**

1059 Pope Nicholas II issues the papal bull *In nomine Domini*, placing papal elections in the hands of cardinal bishops, rather than in those of the Emperor and the lay aristocracy; this decree marks the implementation of a new standardized method of papal selection. [**Europe: Italy**]

1066 The Normans invade England under William the Conqueror, the last successful invasion in British history. [**Europe: United Kingdom of Great Britain and Northern Ireland (England)**]

1071 The Byzantine Empire loses much of Asia Minor to the Saljuq (Seljuk) Turks at the Battle of Manzikert, with the result that Asia Minor becomes largely a Muslim territory and has remained so ever since. [**Asia: Turkey**]

1075 Pope Gregory VII forbids the practice of lay investiture (i.e. the bestowal of a ring and staff by a lay ruler upon a bishop or abbot, symbolizing the clergy's dependence on the local princes). [**Europe: Italy**]

1076 A letter from Pope Gregory VII notes that Bishop Cyriacus of Carthage is the last remaining bishop in Africa; the last Christian epigraphy in North Africa also dates from this time. [**Africa: Tunisia**]

1076–1077 Pope Gregory VII excommunicates the Holy Roman Emperor, Henry IV, following a bitter dispute over the issue of papal versus imperial authority; Henry is compelled to dress in penitential garb and to wait barefoot in the midwinter snow at the Castle of Canossa for three days, before being allowed to enter and beg absolution from Pope Gregory VII. [**Europe: Italy**]

1084 Bruno of Cologne founds a Catholic religious order of enclosed monks, the Carthusians, at Chartreuse in the lower French Alps. [**Europe: France**]

1085 The Conquest of Toledo by King Alfonso VI of Léon marks the first step in the Reconquista (the Christian reconquest of the Iberian Peninsula). [**Europe: Spain**]

1088 The recognition of the University of Bologna by Pope Urban II makes it the first university to be established in Europe. [**Europe: Italy**]

1091 The Normans, under King Roger I of Sicily, capture Malta and are welcomed by the island's Catholic population, who had retained their faith (dating back to the Apostle Paul) under tolerant Muslim occupation since 870. [**Europe: Malta**]

A Timeline of Global Christianity

1095 Pope Urban II preaches the First Crusade at the Council of Clermont; this Crusade is initially in the form of a popular pilgrimage to the Holy Land, but later becomes a military expedition to free Asia Minor, Jerusalem, and the Holy Land from Muslim control. [**Europe: France**]

1098 Anselm of Canterbury writes his *Cur Deus Homo? (Why God Became Man?)*, marking the beginnings of scholastic theology and of Western interpretations of the atonement. [**Europe: Italy, United Kingdom of Great Britain and Northern Ireland (England)**]

1099 The Crusaders capture Jerusalem after a prolonged siege and subject its Muslim and Jewish inhabitants to an appalling massacre in which more than forty thousand are believed to have perished. [**Asia: State of Palestine**]

1114 Despite an almost total Muslim dominance in North Africa, a Christian community survives at Al Qal'a of Beni Hammad, the first capital of the Hammamid emirs. [**Africa: Algeria**]

1122 The Holy Roman Emperor Henry V and Pope Callixtus II sign the Concordat of Worms, ending the long-standing controversy over "simony" and lay investiture. [**Europe: Germany**]

1123 Asser Thorkilsen, the Archbishop of Lund (in the province of Skåne, southern Sweden, but then part of Denmark) ordains Arnaldur as the first bishop of Garðar, on the southern tip of Greenland; Arnaldur arrives at his see in 1126. [**Europe: Denmark, Greenland**]

1130–1155 The involvement of Cistercian monks from southern Europe contributes to the final establishment of Christianity in Sweden during the reign of Sverker. [**Europe: Sweden**]

1145 The German chronicler Otto of Freising makes the first documented reference to the Prester John legend of a Christian kingdom in Asia or Africa, ruled by a priest or "Prester"; this legend is later linked to the Christian king of the Keraits, Toghrul Wang-Khan. [**Asia: Mongolia**]

1146 Pope Eugenius III and King Louis VII of France induce the Cistercian monk Bernard of Clairvaux to preach a Second Crusade to free the Holy Land from Muslim control; Bernard's powerful oratory and passionate sermons motivate his hearers to enlist en masse, with castles and cities often being left empty of able-bodied men as a result. [**Europe: France**]

1147 Pope Eugenius III extends the previously granted indulgences for the Second Crusade to a northern Wendish Crusade, launched to achieve the conversion of the Polabian Slavs (or Wends), one of the last pockets of European paganism; although this is largely unsuccessful, the imposition of Christianity is finally enforced there by the Teutonic Knights in the thirteenth century. [**Europe: Germany, Poland**]

1152 Cardinal Nicholas Breakspear (later to become Pope Adrian IV, the only Briton to occupy the papal throne) establishes the Archbishopric of Nidaros, thus giving the Norwegian church its own archbishopric, rather than it being subject to the Danish archbishopric of Lund. [**Europe: Norway**]

1155 King Erik IX of Sweden carries out a crusade against the Finns, demanding that they be baptized. [**Europe: Finland**]

ca.1157 Peter Lombard completes his theological treatise *Libri Quattuor Sententiarum* (*The Four Books of Sentences*) in Paris; these *Sentences* provide a framework for the theological and philosophical discussions of other thinkers. [**Europe: France**]

1170 Acting on the words attributed to King Henry II ("Will no one rid me of this turbulent priest?"), four knights assassinate Archbishop Thomas à Becket in Canterbury Cathedral; this event forms the basis of T. S. Eliot's verse drama *Murder in the Cathedral*, first performed in 1935. [**Europe: United Kingdom of Great Britain and Northern Ireland (England)**]

1176 The *Liber Censuum Romanae Ecclesiae* (*Census Book of the Roman Church*), the authoritative financial record of the real estate revenues of the papacy from 492 to 1192, makes the last reference to Carthage as an episcopal see; no further Carthaginian bishops are known after this date. [**Africa: Tunisia**]

1179 The Waldenses (a "back to the Bible" movement) emerge in Southern France; however, the Catholic Church strongly opposes the movement for its failure to submit to episcopal authority and excommunicates its adherents the following year. [**Europe: France**]

1187 The Sunni Kurdish general Ṣalāḥ-al-dīn Yūsof ibn Ayyūb (Saladin) reconquers Jerusalem, allowing the defeated Crusaders to leave the city in peace and, in striking contrast to the Crusaders eighty-eight years previously, treating Christian refugees with mercy and compassion. [**Asia: State of Palestine**]

1195 Pope Celestine III proclaims a Northern Crusade against the resistant Baltic heathens around the southern and eastern shores of the Baltic; as part of this crusade, Bishop Berthold of Hanover arrives in Livonia (part of modern-day Latvia) in 1198, seeking to compel the conversion of its inhabitants to Christianity. [**Europe: Latvia**]

1198–1216 The reign of Pope Innocent III marks the high point of papal power in Europe; as the "vicar of Christ" he claims the right to intervene in secular affairs on a large scale, enforcing his will by the use of excommunication (the removal of an individual's access to the Eucharist, and hence to grace and salvation) and the interdict (an "ecclesiastical lockout," which bans all public worship or performance of the Sacraments in any kingdom whose monarch would not obey the papal commands). [**Europe: Italy**]

1204 Pope Innocent III launches the Fourth Crusade, but its diversion to, and sacking of, Constantinople (followed by the setting up of a Latin Patriarchate there), permanently fractures relations between the Byzantine Empire and the West. [**Asia: Turkey**]

1206 Genghis Khan begins the Mongol Conquests across Asia and Eastern Europe; these reach their greatest westward extent in 1241 with the Mongol armies at the gates of Vienna. [**Asia: China, Kazakhstan, Mongolia; Europe: Austria, Belarus, Hungary, Romania, Russian Federation, Ukraine**]

1210 St. Francis of Assisi founds the Franciscan order, also known as the Ordo Fratrum Minorum (i.e. the Little Brothers, OFM), with an emphasis on apostolic poverty and mission. [**Europe: Italy**]

1215 The Fourth Lateran Council convenes as the largest Ecumenical Council to date (with an attendance of seventy-one patriarchs and metropolitan bishops, 412 bishops, more than eight hundred abbots and priors, and at least eight royal ambassadors); the Council defines the Seven Sacraments and passes other decrees for the reform of the Church, the instruction of the clergy and the laity, the suppression of heresy, and a call for a new Crusade. [**Europe: Italy**]

1216 Dominic de Guzman founds the Dominican order, a mendicant religious order dedicated to preaching the Gospel and to opposing heresy (hence its official title of Ordo Praedicatorum, i.e. the Order of Preachers, OP). [**Europe: Italy**]

1219 St. Francis of Assisi goes to Egypt on a peace-making mission, crossing the Crusader-Saracen battle lines at Damietta to preach to Sultan al-Malek al-Kāmel Nāṣer-al-dīn of Egypt, but without success. [**Africa: Egypt**]

1219 The consecration of St. Sava, the greatest of the Serbian national saints, as the autocephalous archbishop of Serbia, strengthens that church's ecclesiastical allegiance to Constantinople, which lasts until the fall of Constantinople to the Turks in 1453 and the de facto abolition of the Patriarchate ten years after that. [**Europe: Bosnia and Herzegovina, Croatia, Montenegro, Serbia**]

1220 Berard of Carbio OFM and four other Franciscan friars go to Spain, Portugal, and North Africa to preach to the Muslims, but are martyred in Marrakesh, Morocco. [**Africa: Morocco**]

1227 After entering Ukraine (then a buffer zone between Catholic and Orthodox spheres of influence) six years earlier, Dominican missionaries convert and baptize its ruler, Prince Bort; a Hungarian Dominican is then appointed as the first Ukrainian bishop the following year. [**Europe: Ukraine**]

1232 Pope Gregory IX establishes the papal Inquisition to prevent allegations of heresy becoming the catalyst for mob violence and to bring a systematic uniformity and legality to the ways in which these accusations are handled. [**Europe: Italy**]

1242 Alexander Nevsky defeats the Teutonic Knights' invasion of Russia at Lake Peipus, when the heavily armored invaders fall through the ice on the northern part of the lake; this enables Russia to remain Orthodox. [**Europe: Estonia, Russian Federation**]

1244 The Khwarezmian Muslim armies, previously driven out of Persia by the Mongols, achieve the final recapture of Jerusalem from the Crusaders. [**Asia: State of Palestine**]

1245–1247 Franciscan friar John of Plano Carpini travels to Mongolia bearing two letters from Pope Innocent IV to Kublai Khan; his journey marks the beginning of a century of Catholic missions to the Mongols. [**Asia: Mongolia**]

1250 The Mamlūks, a non-Arab knightly "slave soldier" caste, seize power in Egypt from the Ayyubid dynasty, adopting a hostile stance toward the Coptic Christians, and decisively advancing the Islamization of Egypt. [**Africa: Egypt**]

ca.1251 The baptism of King Mindowe of Lithuania leads to the provision of a bishop for Lithuania, but Christianity vanishes from the country after Mindowe's death in 1268. [**Europe: Lithuania**]

1252 Sorqaqtani-Beki, the influential Kerait Nestorian Christian princess, dies; she is the daughter-in-law of Genghis Khan (the Great Khan of the Mongols) and the mother of four sons, three of whom became Khan in succession. [**Asia: Mongolia**]

1258 The Mongols under the Il-Khan Hülegü sack Baghdād and bring about the end of the 'Abbasid Caliphate in Iraq; the commander of Hülegü's advance guard is a Nestorian general, Ked-Buka. [**Asia: Iraq**]

1260 The Mamlūk Muslim armies turn the Mongol invaders back at the Battle of 'Ayn Jālūt in Galilee; this successful defense marks a significant turning point in world history. [**Asia: State of Palestine**]

1261 Byzantine general Alexios Komnenos Strategopoulos recaptures Constantinople from the Latin Crusaders by means of a commando attack on the city through a secret passage and restores Byzantine rule. [**Asia: Turkey**]

1265–1266 Marco Polo's father and uncle (Niccolò and Maffeo) become the first Europeans known to have reached China, arriving in Kublai Khan's summer capital Shangtu (Xanadu), 350 kilometers north of Beijing (previous travelers, e.g. John of Plano Carpini and William of Rubruck, are only able to journey as far as Outer Mongolia). [**Asia: China**]

1272 Dawud I, the Christian king of Makouria, launches an unwise attack on the Egyptian Red Sea seaport of Aidhab (despite the terms of the *baqt* treaty with its rulers), leading to a retaliatory invasion under Mamlūk Sultan Baybars. [**Africa: Sudan**]

1274 Thomas Aquinas, the greatest of the medieval Scholastic theologians, dies, leaving his sixty-one-volume *Summa Theologiae* unfinished. [**Europe: Italy**]

1275 The Polo brothers return to China, this time with Marco Polo, who observes numerous Nestorian communities along the Silk Road and in China; he spends sixteen years there before returning home ca.1291. [**Asia: China**]

1275 Two young Mongol Nestorian monks, Mark and Ṣaumā, set out from Peking on a pilgrimage to Jerusalem, eventually reaching the Court of the Nestorian Patriarch Denha at Marabegh in Azerbaijan. [**Asia: Azerbaijan, China**]

1279 Mamlūk repression intensifies toward the Coptic Christians, with forty-four churches being destroyed in Cairo alone between 1279 and 1447. [**Africa: Egypt**]

1281 The Church of the East chooses the Mongol Nestorian monk Mark (despite his inability to speak Syriac, the language of the church) as Patriarch Yaballaha III to succeed Denha and enthrones him at Mār Koka near Baghdād. [**Asia: Iraq**]

1287 The Il-Khan Arġūn sends the Mongol monk Ṣaumā (by now a Nestorian bishop) from Iran on an ambassadorial mission to the pope and to the Christian Courts of Europe; as part of this mission, Ṣaumā visits Rome, Paris, and Gascony (where he celebrates Mass for the English King, Edward I). [**Asia: Islamic Republic of Iran (Persia); Europe: France, Italy**]

1289 As part of his policy of maintaining an impartial religious balance, Kublai Khan creates a *chung-fu-ssu* (department) of the Chinese government to administer the affairs of the increasing numbers of Christians in his empire, appointing the Nestorian physician Ai-hsueh as its head. [**Asia: China**]

1291 The appointment of Magnus, the first indigenous bishop of Åbo, marks the completion of the official Christianization of Finland. [**Europe: Finland**]

1293 The Catalan mystic and poet Ramon Llull makes the first of his missionary journeys to Tunis. [**Africa: Tunisia**]

ca.1300 The Armenian monk Abu Salih records the existence of several Nestorian churches at "Fanshur" (probably Barus) in West Sumatra. [**Asia: Indonesia**]

A Timeline of Global Christianity

1302 Pope Boniface VIII issues his bull *Unam Sanctam*; this is one of the most extreme claims to papal authority ever made, stating the superiority of the spiritual power over the secular order and claiming universal papal jurisdiction: ". . . we declare, state, define, and pronounce that it is altogether necessary to salvation for every human creature to be subject to the Roman pontiff [i.e. the pope]." **[Europe: Italy]**

1305–1377 The Avignon Captivity of the papacy begins with the election of the French Pope Clement V, who declines to travel to Rome and relocates the papal Court to Avignon in 1309, where it remains for the next sixty-seven years. **[Europe: France]**

1315 The Muslim government of Egypt installs a Nubian Muslim as King Saif ad-Dīn 'Abdullah Bershambo of Makouria, thus making the country officially Muslim. **[Africa: Sudan]**

1317 The conversion of the Cathedral in Dongola, the capital of Makouria, into a mosque contributes to the extinction of Christianity there. **[Africa: Sudan]**

1318 'Abdisho' bar Brika of Nisibis (also known in Latin as Ebed-Jesu) refers to a Syrian metropolitan bishop of "Ṣīn [northern China], Māṣīn [southern China], and Dābag [southern Sumatra]." **[Asia: China, Indonesia]**

1318 A Nestorian synod meets in Persia for the enthronement of a new patriarch (Timothy II) following the death of Yaballaha III; although there may have been subsequent patriarchs, this is the last recorded synod of the Nestorian Church of the East. **[Asia: Islamic Republic of Iran (Persia)]**

1337 The Ethiopian church begins a period of aggressive evangelization by force of arms as part of a pursuit of cultural hegemony by the Ethiopian warrior king Amda-Simon. **[Africa: Djibouti, Ethiopia, (Somaliland)]**

ca.1340 The famous Russian ascetic, spiritual leader, and monastic reformer Sergii of Radonezh founds the Trinity Lavra of St. Sergius, the most significant Russian monastery and the spiritual center of the Russian Orthodox Church; Sergii is today seen as "Russia's patron saint." **[Europe: Russian Federation]**

1346 Giovanni de Marignolli, the last resident Catholic bishop in China until the end of the Middle Ages, reports finding Christians in the

Majapahit royal court of Queen Regent Tribhuwanottunggadewī Jayawiṣṇuwardhanī in East Java on his journey home by sea to Europe. [**Asia: Indonesia**]

1346–1349 The Black Death, carried by means of rat-borne infected fleas along the overland and maritime trade routes from China, devastates Europe, with a death toll of a third to a half of the population in some areas. [**Europe**]

1368 The Mongol Yuan dynasty falls and the xenophobic Confucian Ming Dynasty comes to power, leading to a declining interest in Christianity; this drop in influence is compounded by division between Nestorians and Catholics in China. [**Asia: China**]

By 1370 The Mongol Emperor Tamerlane gains control of the western Chagatai Khanate and launches ferocious attacks across Asia from his base in Samarkand, slaughtering an estimated seventeen million people (both Christians and Muslims); these genocidal attacks almost completely destroy the church of the East. [**Asia: Uzbekistan**]

1378 Catherine of Siena attempts to persuade Pope Gregory XI to return the papal Court from Avignon to Rome. [**Europe: Italy**]

1378 The papal Great Schism develops, with two rival claimants to the papacy (Urban VI and Clement VII); the Schism intensifies with the appointment of a third pope (Alexander V) by the Council of Pisa in 1409. [**Europe: France, Italy, Germany**]

1384 The English Reformer John Wycliffe, known as "the Morning Star of the Reformation," dies; forty-four years after his death, his bones are exhumed and burnt as those of a heretic by his enemies, but as seventeenth-century churchman Thomas Fuller later wrote: "They burned his bones to ashes and cast them into the Swift, a neighboring brook running hard by. Thus the brook conveyed his ashes into the Avon, the Avon into the Severn, the Severn into the narrow seas and they into the main ocean. And so the ashes of Wycliffe are symbolic of his doctrine, which is now spread throughout the world." [**Europe: United Kingdom of Great Britain and Northern Ireland (England)**]

1386 Lithuania formally becomes Christian as a result of a marriage between the royal families of Lithuania and Poland. [**Europe: Lithuania**]

1414 Despite having already been excommunicated for heresy, the Bohemian reformer Jan Hus attends the Council of Constance under a guarantee of safe conduct, but this is rescinded on the grounds that "the Church does not keep faith with heretics," and he is arrested, and burnt at the stake the following year. [**Europe: Czechia (Czech Republic), Germany**]

1414–1418 The Council of Constance deposes the three rival claimants to the papal throne and elects Oddone Colonna as Pope Martin V; in so doing it demonstrates that general councils have greater authority than the popes. [**Europe: Germany**]

1415 The Portuguese make a surprise assault across the Straits of Gibraltar to seize Ceuta, thereby gaining their first foothold in Africa, which is later taken over by Spain; this attack marks the beginning of European colonialism in Africa. [**Africa: (Ceuta)**]

1416 The Portuguese Prince Henry "the Navigator" initiates voyages of exploration down the coast of West Africa; these are made possible by the invention of the caravel, a newer, lighter, and more maneuverable sailing vessel with lateen sails, which could travel further and faster, as well as sail "into the wind." [**Africa: Cabo Verde, Gambia, Guinea, Guinea-Bissau, Mauritania, Senegal, Sierra Leone, Western Sahara**]

1418 Thomas à Kempis, a German-Dutch Canon Regular and a member of the Devotio Moderna (Modern Devotion) spiritual movement, publishes his devotional book *De Imitatio Christi* (*Concerning the Imitation of Christ*); this became a widely used handbook for the spiritual life, with the current number of editions up to the present day now standing at more than two thousand. [**Europe: Netherlands**]

1431–1449 The Seventeenth Ecumenical Council of the Roman Catholic Church, held in several stages at Basel, Ferrara, and Florence, seeks to heal the rift between the Roman and Byzantine churches. [**Europe: Italy, Switzerland**]

1432 The Portuguese king Afonso V begins his reign; he is known as "the African" for his military campaigns and conquests in Morocco, which mark the beginnings of Portuguese exploration and expansion in Africa. [**Africa: Morocco**]

1434 The Portuguese explorer Gil Eanes reaches Cape Bojador on the coast of West Africa, a significant milestone in the European exploration of Africa. [**Africa: Western Sahara**]

1435 Pope Eugene IV's papal bull *Sicut Dudum* forbids the enslavement of the native peoples in the Canary Islands, but this is ignored by the Spanish colonizers. [**Africa: (Canary Islands)**]

1436 The Emperor Zara' Ya'eqob reforms the Ethiopian Church and attempts to resolve its long-running Sabbatarian controversy, although this schism does not end until 1450. [**Africa: Ethiopia**]

1439 Pope Eugene IV invites the Coptic Patriarch John XI to attend the Ecumenical Council of Florence in an attempt to reestablish contact between the Catholic and the Coptic Churches. [**Africa: Egypt**]

1448 A council of Russian bishops installs Jonas, the bishop of Ryazan and Murom, as Metropolitan of Moscow and of all Russia; Jonas's installation (without reference to the Ecumenical Patriarch of Constantinople, who normally made this appointment) marks the beginnings of a de facto Russian independence from Constantinople. [**Europe: Russian Federation**]

1450s Johannes Gutenberg invents the printing press, with the first mass-produced book printed with movable type in Europe being the Latin Vulgate Bible in 1455. [**Europe: Germany**]

1453 Constantinople falls to Sultan Muḥammad II and the Ottoman Turks, who kill the Emperor Constantine XI and bring the Eastern Roman (Byzantine) Empire to an end after more than eleven hundred years. [**Asia: Turkey**]

1479 The Catholic monarchs Ferdinand II of Aragón and Isabella I of Castile establish the Spanish Inquisition, to examine the orthodoxy of those who had converted from Judaism and Islam to Catholicism in their territories. [**Europe: Spain**]

1482 A Portuguese expedition under Diogo de Azambuja constructs the Castelo of São Jorge da Mina (the Castle of St. George of the Mine), the oldest European building south of the Sahara, at Elmina on the Gold Coast as a fortified base for trading with the whole of West Africa; although this base also has a missionary focus, its resident chaplains are primarily concerned with the European enclave and had little impact on African peoples. [**Africa: Ghana**]

1483 Portuguese ships arrive off the coast of Kongo, beginning a Catholic mission that survives, in indigenized form, until the late nineteenth century. [**Africa: Angola, Congo, Democratic Republic of the Congo**]

1491 The baptisms of Nzinga a Nkuwu (who takes the title of King João I of Kongo) and of his son, Mvemba a Nzinga (who becomes king Afonso I in 1506), lead to their patronage of the Catholic mission in Kongo until 1543. [**Africa: Angola, Congo, Democratic Republic of the Congo**]

1492 Christopher Columbus discovers the Americas on behalf of Ferdinand II of Aragón and Isabella I of Castile, making his first landfall in the Bahamas. [**Latin America and the Caribbean: Bahamas**]

1492 The Muslim kingdom of Grenada, the last outpost of Moorish rule, falls to the kingdom of Castile, and the last Muslims are expelled from Spain, completing the Reconquista (the reconquest of the Iberian Peninsula). [**Europe: Spain**]

1493-1494 Pope Alexander VI issues the bull *Inter caetera* in 1493, allocating all discoveries in the New World west and south of a line drawn west of the Azores to Castile; this line is moved 270 leagues westward in the Treaty of Tordesillas between Castile and Portugal the following year, thereby inadvertently including Brazil (but not other New World territories) in the Portuguese, rather than the Spanish, sphere of influence. [**Latin America and the Caribbean: Brazil; Europe: Portugal, Spain**]

1494 The Portuguese explorer Pero da Covilhão arrives in Ethiopia and claims that its emperor Eskender was Prester John; however, da Covilhão is not permitted to leave Ethiopia and dies there thirty years later. [**Africa: Ethiopia**]

1498 The Dominican friar Girolamo Savanarola preaches renewal in Florence, where his extreme puritanism is exemplified by his "bonfires of the vanities" (the burning of objects such as art, cosmetics, and books, deemed by authorities to be occasions of sin); paradoxically Savanarola himself is later burned at the stake. [**Europe: Italy**]

1498 Vasco da Gama sails around Africa and reaches India, thereby initiating the era of European expansion and colonization in Asia; Catholic missionaries accompany him on his second expedition in 1503. [**Asia: India**]

1500 Despite the eclipse of Christianity in neighboring Makouria 183 years earlier, the Christian kingdom of Alwa appears to have survived until about 1500, although a successor Islamic state is founded in 1504. [**Africa: Sudan**]

1500 The Portuguese explorer Pedro Álvares Cabral discovers Brazil and makes friendly contact with the local inhabitants; men from his ship build a Christian altar and celebrate the first mass in Brazil four days after his arrival. [**Latin America and the Caribbean: Brazil**]

1501 The Spanish Franciscan priest Francisco Garcia de Padilla OFM arrives in Santo Domingo as the first bishop in Hispaniola (the name given to the island now comprising Haiti and the Dominican Republic). [**Latin America and the Caribbean: Dominican Republic, Haiti**]

1506 Pope Julius II lays the foundation stone of St. Peter's in Rome; the fund-raising required for this massive rebuilding project and for the papal sponsorship of Renaissance art reinforces resentment (particularly in Germany) at the extravagance of the papacy, contributing to the emergence of the Reformation. [**Europe: Italy**]

1510 Italian adventurer Lodovico de Varthema reports meeting some Nestorians in Malacca from refugee communities in Thailand and claims that the ruler of Pegu (lower Myanmar) had thousands of Christians in his service; however, this identification appears to be due to de Varthema's misinterpretation of the Buddhist "Three Jewels" (or "Three Refuges") of Buddha, Sangha, and Dharma as equivalents of the Christian Trinity. [**Asia: Malaysia, Myanmar (Burma), Thailand**]

1510 Moscow declares itself to be the "Third Rome" (i.e. the successor as head of the Church after the Fall of Rome in 410 and of Constantinople in 1453). [**Europe: Russian Federation**]

1510 The first Dominicans arrive in Hispaniola, followed by a party of two thousand five hundred settlers the following year. [**Latin America and the Caribbean: Dominican Republic, Haiti**]

1511 The Dominican priest Antonio de Montesinos preaches against the encomienda (entrusting) system, requiring groups of Indians to render tribute and services to individual adventurers; de Montesinos insists that the cruel and unjust treatment of the Indians under this system is tantamount to slavery. [**Latin America and the Caribbean: Dominican Republic, Haiti**]

1511 The Portuguese conquer Malacca, taking it from its Muslim rulers and making it their base for mission and trade in Southeast and East Asia. [**Asia: Malaysia**]

1512-1513 King Frederick II of Aragón and his daughter, Queen Joanna I of Castile, pass the Laws of Burgos protecting the rights of the natives and regulating the settlements in the Americas. [**Latin America and the Caribbean: Dominican Republic, Haiti**]

1513 The Spanish monarchy orders the mandatory reading of the Requerimiento (i.e. "The Requirement": a statement—in Spanish—of Spain's right to conquest) to the natives on a first encounter; this included their obligation to allow preaching to them by Catholic missionaries. [**Latin America and the Caribbean: Dominican Republic, Haiti**]

1513 Vasco Nuñez de Balboa views the Pacific Ocean from the Isthmus of Panama, the first European to do so. [**Latin America and the Caribbean: Panama**]

1514 Bartolomé de Las Casas, the first person to be ordained in the Americas (becoming a priest in 1512 or 1513 and, later, a Dominican friar) develops an increasing opposition to the oppressive encomienda system and thereafter devotes himself to the defense of the Indians. [**Latin America and the Caribbean: Dominican Republic, Haiti**]

1514-1517 Cardinal Jiménez de Cisneros Francisco of Castile initiates the translation of the Complutensian Polyglot Bible as part of an ongoing program of reform within the Spanish monastic orders, clergy, and Church; this Bible contains the Vulgate Latin translation of the Old Testament, the Greek Old Testament (Septuagint) with interlinear Latin, the Hebrew Old Testament, and an Aramaic paraphrase, together with a Latin translation. [**Europe: Spain**]

1515 The first missionaries reach the kingdom of Benin, where accounts of a distant chief monarch to the East, who had sent the newly crowned king of Benin a cross, led them to believe that they had at last found Prester John. [**Africa: Benin**]

1517 Martin Luther draws up the Ninety-Five Theses, kindling the beginnings of the Lutheran Reformation; there is now scholarly debate over whether he actually nailed these Theses on the church door at Wittenberg or whether he simply sent them to the Church authorities. [**Europe: Germany**]

1517 The Ottoman Turks occupy Egypt, cutting off contacts between the Coptic Church and the West for more than a century. [**Africa: Egypt**]

1519–1521 The Spanish conquistador Hernán Cortés de Monroy y Pizarro Altamirano attacks and conquers the Aztecs in Mexico. [**Latin America and the Caribbean: Mexico**]

1520 Dom Henrique, the brother of King Afonso I of Kongo, becomes the titular bishop of the province of Utica (Tunisia) and, as such, the first African Catholic bishop. [**Africa: Angola, Congo, Democratic Republic of the Congo**]

1521 A Spanish expedition, led by the Portuguese captain Ferñao de Magalhães (Ferdinand Magellan), becomes the first group of European explorers to enter the Pacific Ocean during their circumnavigation of the globe; during this voyage, Magellan is killed in a tribal skirmish on the island of Mactan in the Philippines. [**Asia: Philippines; Oceania**]

1521 Martin Luther appears before Emperor Charles V at the Diet of Worms, where he is condemned for his views but remains steadfast, reported as famously saying "I cannot and I will not recant anything. . . . Here I stand; I cannot do otherwise. God help me. Amen." [**Europe: Germany**]

1522 Zwingli's support for the proponents in the "Affair of the Sausages" (during which a number of his colleagues had consumed a meal of sausages during Lent, thus breaking the pre-Easter fast) brings the Swiss Reformation into the open. [**Europe: Switzerland**]

1523 A letter from the Spanish Crown to the Spanish conquistador Hernán Cortés de Monroy y Pizarro Altamirano forbids the oppression of the Indians in the Americas. [**Latin America and the Caribbean: Mexico**]

1524 Twelve Franciscan missionaries arrive in Mexico and begin work, followed by twelve Dominicans the following year. [**Latin America and the Caribbean: Mexico**]

1524–1525 More than a century of agrarian unrest in Germany culminates in the outbreak of the Peasants' War; the radical Reformation preaching of Thomas Müntzer adds a religious dimension to this social revolt. [**Europe: Germany**]

1525 William Tyndale publishes his translation of the New Testament, the first to be printed in English, at Cologne and Worms, in defiance of the 1408 Constitutions of Oxford, which strictly forbade translations of the Bible into the native tongue. [**Europe: Germany, United Kingdom of Great Britain and Northern Ireland (England)**]

1526–1529 After the conquest of Hungary, the Muslim armies under Suleiman the Magnificent advance toward Vienna in a great invasion of Islam into Christendom; their military successes are seen by Christians as an apocalyptic sign of the end of the world. [**Europe: Austria, Hungary**]

1527 The Synod of Schleitheim formulates the "Schleitheim Articles," a doctrinal agreement summarizing the key features of the Brüderliche Vereinigung (Swiss Brethren) movement; these include (among others) the baptism of adult believers by full immersion (hence the name "Anabaptists" or "rebaptizers"), separation from the world, and the prohibition of the bearing of arms or the swearing of oaths. [**Europe: Switzerland**]

1529 The Second Diet of Speyer, convened to formulate action against the Turks (then besieging Vienna) and to halt the progress of the Lutheran reformation, orders that Catholicism be followed in all states of the Holy Roman Empire; the Lutheran princes at the Diet issue a legal appeal or "protest" against this ruling, their action creating the label of "Protestant." [**Europe: Germany**]

1530s Both Sao Tome and Cabo Verde become independent Catholic dioceses and for several centuries provide priests at irregular intervals for the African mainland. [**Africa: Cabo Verde, Sao Tome and Principe**]

1531 Juan de Zumárraga, the first bishop-elect of Mexico, reports that he had presided over the demolition of five hundred temples and twenty-six thousand idols; this report may have been an attempt to justify his activities as bishop and Protector of the Indians, since he had not yet been consecrated. [**Latin America and the Caribbean: Mexico**]

1531 Spanish prelate Diego Alvarez de Osorio serves as the first bishop-elect in Nicaragua, although he is never actually consecrated into this office. [**Latin America and the Caribbean: Nicaragua**]

1531 Vicente Pegado, captain of the Portuguese river garrison of Sofala in Mozambique, records accounts of the ruined city of Great Zimbabwe, which apparently had been abandoned about 1450. [**Africa: Zimbabwe**]

1531 Visions of Our Lady of Guadalupe, fusing Indian indigenous and European elements, appear to two Nahuatl peasants. [**Latin America and the Caribbean: Mexico**]

1531–1543 Islamic jihāds from the neighboring state of Adal destroy monasteries, churches, and libraries in Ethiopia, but Portuguese help arrives in 1541, leading to the defeat of the Muslim general Imām Aḥmad ibn Ibrāhim al-Ghāzi. [**Africa: Ethiopia**]

1534 Despite its vigorous growth under the patronage of the Kongolese Christian king Afonso I (Mvemba a Nzinga), the pope places the church in the Kongo under the bishopric of Sao Tome, thus maintaining Portuguese rights of control under the *patronado* (system of patronage); despite the steady export of Kongolese slaves to Sao Tome, this episcopal control would remain in place until 1596. [**Africa: Angola, Congo, Democratic Republic of the Congo, Sao Tome and Principe**]

1534 King Henry VIII asserts the supremacy of the English sovereign (rather than the pope) over the Church of England, thus initiating the English Reformation. [**Europe: United Kingdom of Great Britain and Northern Ireland (England)**]

1534 The first Catholic missionaries arrive in Celebes and the Moluccas, although the first Catholic baptisms are not performed by them, but by Gonzalo Veloso, a Portuguese trader on the island of Halmahera in the Northern Moluccas. [**Asia: Indonesia**]

1534–1535 A militant Radical Anabaptist group seizes power at Munster and sets up a millennial community of the Elect under John of Leyden ("the King of New Zion"), but are besieged by forces loyal to the exiled Catholic bishop, and ruthlessly killed. [**Europe: Germany**]

1536 John Calvin publishes the original Latin edition of his seminal *Institutes of the Christian Religion* in Basel; the definitive extended edition would be published in Geneva in 1559. [**Europe: Switzerland**]

1537 Portuguese trader Jurdão de Freitas influences Tabarija, the exiled king of the Moluccas, to convert to Christianity in the Portuguese colony of Goa (India); Tabarija thus becomes the first Christian king in the East Indies. [**Asia: Indonesia**]

1537 Spanish priest Vasco de Quiroga becomes the bishop of Michoacán and sets up a utopian community for the Indians in his diocese. [**Latin America and the Caribbean: Mexico**]

1537 The papal bull *Sublimis Deus* of Pope Paul III defends the rights of the Indians in the Americas, but this decree is ignored by the Spanish conquistadores. [**Latin America and the Caribbean**]

1540 A group of plotters (including some Portuguese residents) attempt to assassinate King Afonso I at an Easter Day service, in response to his opposition to the Portuguese-controlled slave trade. [**Africa: Angola, Congo, Democratic Republic of the Congo**]

1540 Although early missionaries had used force to convert the Peruvian Indians up to 1540, the Council of Lima advocates their conversion through the teaching of the faith; this becomes the Jesuits' standard practice after 1569. [**Latin America and the Caribbean: Peru**]

1540 Pope Paul III authorizes Ignatius Loyola's Society of Jesus (Jesuits) as a missionary order professing vows of poverty, chastity, and special obedience to the pope in matters of mission direction and assignment. [**Europe: Italy**]

1541 John Calvin begins his program of civic and religious reform in Geneva through the City Council's enactment of his Ecclesiastical Ordinances; these measures establish the "Four Ministries" (pastors, doctors [i.e. teachers of Scripture], elders, and deacons), and set up the Consistory as an ecclesiastical court to systematically supervise the morals of the people of Geneva, with the intention of making the town a disciplined community, living in conformity with the Gospel. [**Europe: Switzerland**]

1541 The Diet of Regensburg brings together Catholics (led by Cardinal Gasparo Contarini) and Protestants (represented by Martin Bucer, Philip Melancthon, and others) in theological debate, marking the culmination of attempts to restore religious unity in the Holy Roman Empire. [**Europe: Germany**]

1542 Francis Xavier begins work in Goa, officially as the papal Nuncio and also as the commissioner of the king of Portugal, but refuses the trappings of office for the sake of his mission. [**Asia: India**]

1542 The Spanish government passes two laws reforming the whole system of encomienda (requiring groups of Indians to render tribute and services to individual adventurers), which had resulted in the abuse of the native populations; these new laws prohibit their enslavement and grant Native Americans specific protections. [**Latin America and the Caribbean**]

1543 Although half of Kongo's population of four million had by now become Christian, a large Portuguese-controlled trade continues in slaves (many of whom also were Christian) with the Americas. [**Africa: Angola, Congo, Democratic Republic of the Congo**]

1543 The Buddhist king Buvanaika Bahu VII of Kotte requests King João III of Portugal to send Catholic missionaries to Sri Lanka; six Franciscans and their superior arrive in 1546 and build a church at Colombo. [**Asia: Sri Lanka**]

1545 Xavier arrives in Malacca, where he works for three months to halt the moral depravity of the city (known as the "Sodom and Gomorrah of the East" because of the lifestyles of its Portuguese and Malay inhabitants). [**Asia: Malaysia**]

1545–1563 The important Council of Trent begins, with the intentions of countering the Protestants, bringing reform to the Church's discipline and administration, and providing new "Roman" definitions of Catholic doctrine and practice. [**Europe: Italy**]

1546 The posthumous publication of Polish mathematician-astronomer Nicolaus Copernicus's book *On the Revolutions of the Celestial Spheres* (in which he sets out his heliocentric theory of the movements of the planets, in opposition to the Church-sanctioned Ptolemaic earth-centered model) stimulates a "Paradigm Shift" in the way in which the universe is viewed, thus making an important contribution to the beginnings of the Scientific Revolution. [**Europe: Poland**]

1546–1547 Xavier spends fourteen months in the Moluccas (also known as the "Spice Islands"), preaching on the islands of Amboina (Ambon), Ternate, Halmahera, and Morotai. [**Asia: Indonesia**]

1549 Archbishop Thomas Cranmer publishes the *First Book of Common Prayer*, his 1552 revision removing residual Catholic practices from its liturgy; this is revised again in 1662 after the restoration of the Stuart monarchy and becomes the standard version throughout the British imperial period. [**Europe: United Kingdom of Great Britain and Northern Ireland (England)**]

1549 On his return to Malacca, Xavier encounters Anjiro, a Japanese runaway from criminal justice and launches the first Jesuit mission to Japan, where he has great success, initiating the "Christian Century" (1550–1650) in Japan. [**Asia: Japan**]

1549 The Portuguese king João III sends the first Jesuit mission to Brazil under the leadership of Father Manuel da Nóbrega. [**Latin America and the Caribbean: Brazil**]

1550–1551 The Dominican missionary friar-bishop Bartolomé de las Casas debates with the Spanish humanist scholar Juan Ginés de Sepúlveda in Valladolid, Spain, on the issues of colonialism and the welfare of the Indians. [**Latin America and the Caribbean: Mexico**]

1552 Bartolomé de las Casas publishes a vigorous attack on the treatment of the Indians (*A Short Account of the Destruction of the Indies*), detailing the abuses committed by some Spaniards against them. [**Latin America and the Caribbean: Mexico**]

1552 The first Council of Lima decides to withhold the Eucharist from Indian believers, apparently due to concerns over the perceived superficiality of their conversion (although racial prejudice may also have been a factor). [**Latin America and the Caribbean: Peru**]

1552 Xavier dies of fever on Shang-ch'uan Tao (Sancian Island, off the coast of China near Guangzhou) after failing to enter China. [**Asia: China**]

1553 The Jesuits found a new mission at Luanda (Angola), after being expelled from Kongo following tensions with its King Diogo I Nkumbi a Mpudi. [**Africa: Angola, Congo, Democratic Republic of the Congo**]

1553–1558 Following the death of King Edward VI and the attempted placing of Lady Jane Grey on the throne in order to safeguard Protestant gains, a Catholic reaction takes place in England under Mary Tudor ("Bloody Mary") and Bishops Latimer and Ridley and Archbishop Cranmer are burnt at the stake in 1555 and 1556. [**Europe: United Kingdom of Great Britain and Northern Ireland (England)**]

1554 French Franciscan friar Pierre Bonifer leads a short-lived Catholic mission in Burma, but no enduring Christian presence is created there until the establishment of a Portuguese fort near Pegu from 1600 to 1613. [**Asia: Myanmar (Burma)**]

1555 Dominican missions reach the Eastern Indonesian Archipelago and establish strong Catholic churches in Flores, Solor, and Timor; although Solor is initially the strongest of these communities, that on Timor survives into the twenty-first century, helping to prevent the absorption of East Timor either by Islam or by Indonesian political hegemony. [**Asia: Indonesia, Timor-Leste**]

1555 Nicolas Durand de Villegaignon and Jean de Cointac set up a short-lived French Calvinist Protestant (Huguenot) colony in Rio de Janiero. [**Latin America and the Caribbean: Brazil**]

1555 The first Council of Mexico recommends that Indians, mulattos, and mestizos should not be ordained, although the ordination of half-castes and of illegitimate sons is later allowed by Pope Gregory XIV in 1576. [**Latin America and the Caribbean: Mexico**]

1555 The signing of the Peace of Augsburg provides the first permanent legal basis for the coexistence of Lutheranism and Catholicism in Germany; this politico-religious settlement, based on the formula *Cuius regio, eius religio* ("Whose region, his religion," i.e. the inhabitants of each Prince's realm are to follow that Prince's religion) ends religious conflict in Germany for more than fifty years. [**Europe: Germany**]

1557 The Muslim Ottoman Emperor Suleiman the Magnificent restores the Serbian Patriarchate, vacant since 1463; this assists the unification of the Serbs in the Ottoman Empire, although the Turks again abolish the Patriarchate in 1766. [**Europe: Bosnia and Herzegovina, Croatia, Montenegro, North Macedonia, Serbia**]

1559 Queen Elizabeth I, although favoring the Protestants, seeks to maintain a balance in England between the papal Catholics and the radical

("Puritan") reformers by instituting an inclusive religious settlement for the Church of England in which all parties could claim that their views are maintained; this Elizabethan settlement becomes known as the *via media*, i.e. the "middle way." [**Europe: United Kingdom of Great Britain and Northern Ireland (England)**]

1559 The first national synod of the rapidly growing French Reformed (Huguenot) Churches, held in secret near Paris, approves a Confession of Faith and a Church Discipline, both following the Calvinist model. [**Europe: France**]

1560 The Scottish Parliament passes Acts disestablishing the Roman Church and reforming the Church in Scotland; John Knox influences this activity by preaching a series of sermons, from the book of Haggai on the Rebuilding of the Temple, at public services held outside the High Kirk of Edinburgh (St. Giles's Kirk), adjacent to the Parliament's meeting place in the Old Tolbooth. [**Europe: United Kingdom of Great Britain and Northern Ireland (Scotland)**]

1563 Matthew Parker, Archbishop of Canterbury, prepares the Thirty-Nine Articles (a revision of the earlier Forty-Two Articles of King Edward VI's reign, complemented by Johannes Brenz's Lutheran Confession of Württemberg) as a doctrinal foundation for the Church of England; these Thirty-Nine Articles would be published in their final, official, form in 1571. [**Europe: United Kingdom of Great Britain and Northern Ireland (England)**]

1565 Miguel López de Legazpi establishes the first Spanish colony at Cebu, where Catholic Augustinian missionaries under Andrés de Urdaneta baptize their first convert, the niece of Raja Tupas, the chief of Cebu, later the same year. [**Asia: Philippines**]

1566 Following a temporary suspension of heresy laws in the face of the Dutch nobility's protests against Spanish Catholic rule, thousands of Protestant refugees flock back to the Netherlands, sparking a call for religious freedom and the outbreak of a Calvinist "iconoclast" reformation in the Netherlands. [**Europe: Netherlands**]

1567 Portuguese friars Jeronimo de la Cruz and Sebastião da Canto, the first Dominican missionaries to Thailand, arrive in the Siamese capital of Ayutthia; although they are initially well received, they are also opposed by Muslim agitators and fail to win a single convert, with de la Cruz and two new missionaries being killed in 1569. [**Asia: Thailand**]

1568 Roving bands of Yaka Jaga warriors invade Kongo, destroying San Salvador and burning churches, the king regaining his capital only with Portuguese aid. [**Africa: Angola, Congo, Democratic Republic of the Congo**]

1569 The signing of the Union of Lublin creates a single Polish-Lithuanian Commonwealth; at the same time, Ukraine becomes part of Poland and adopts a completely Catholic official religious identity, leading to the persecution of the Ukrainian Orthodox Church (which had resisted the pressures of Polonization). [**Europe: Ukraine**]

1570 An extensive network of Catholic bishoprics emerges throughout Latin America, linked to the metropolitan sees in Mexico City and Lima. [**Latin America and the Caribbean: Mexico, Peru**]

1570s Christianity arrives in the Niger Delta kingdom of Warri and survives until end of the eighteenth century, despite long periods without missionaries. [**Africa: Nigeria**]

1571 The administrative base of Catholic missions and of colonial settlement in the Philippines moves north from Cebu to Manila, which becomes a suffragan see of Mexico City in 1578; its first resident bishop (Domingo de Salazar) arrives in 1581. [**Asia: Philippines**]

1571 Under the leadership of Bartolomeu Dias's grandson, the Portuguese establish Angola as a private proprietary colony, in a format similar to that of the Virginia colony later set up by the British in the Americas. [**Africa: Angola**]

1572 Believed to have been initiated by Catherine de' Medici, mother of King Charles IX, the St. Bartholomew's Day Massacre of the French Calvinist Protestants (Huguenots) takes place, with more than twenty thousand killed. [**Europe: France**]

1572 Visionary Carmelite nun Teresa of Ávila reaches mystical heights of contemplative prayer, experiencing a "spiritual marriage" to Christ as the bridegroom of the soul. [**Europe: Spain**]

1579 Italian missionary Alessandro Valignano (the leader of all Jesuit missions in Asia) arrives in Japan and insists that all Jesuit missionaries there should learn the Japanese language and fit in with Japanese culture as much as possible. [**Asia: Japan**]

1582 After three years in Japan as Vicar-General of the Jesuit mission, Valignano leaves to set up a base in the Portuguese colony of Macao for sending missionaries into China. [**Asia: China**]

1582 The Jesuit scholar Matteo Ricci arrives in Macao and, because of his brilliant academic reputation, is invited into China the following year by Wang P'an, the governor of Shaoqing, near Guangzhou; Ricci's mission focuses on the conversion of Chinese scholars and of the upper classes. [**Asia: China**]

1587 After initially favoring the Christians, the Kampaku (Regent) Toyotomi Hideyoshi issues a short-lived Anti-Christian Edict ordering the missionaries to leave the country within twenty days and all their Japanese converts to recant. [**Asia: Japan**]

1587 The Jesuits arrive in Paraguay to begin work, although their mission to the Indians does not start in earnest until 1609. [**Latin America and the Caribbean: Paraguay**]

1589 The Ecumenical Patriarch Jeremias II of Constantinople visits Moscow, leading to its recognition as the fifth patriarchate of the Orthodox Church. [**Europe: Russian Federation**]

1592 Japan invades Korea with an army which includes eighteen thousand Christian soldiers; at the end of the following year, Spanish Jesuit Gregorio de Cespedes accompanies them as their chaplain, in the process becoming one of the first Westerners to visit Korea. [**Asia: Democratic People's Republic of Korea (North Korea), Republic of Korea (South Korea)**]

1596 Andrew Melville's forthright remark to King James VI sums up the attitudes of the Scottish Reformation: "There are two kings and two kingdoms in Scotland. There is Christ Jesus the King and His kingdom the Kirk [Church], whose subject King James the Sixth is, and of whose kingdom not a king, nor a lord, nor a head, but a member." [**Europe: United Kingdom of Great Britain and Northern Ireland (Scotland)**]

1596 Rome makes San Salvador (Kongo) a see in its own right in order to break the Portuguese monopoly on religion in the area. [**Africa: Angola, Congo, Democratic Republic of the Congo**]

1596 The Dominicans become the dominant mission on the islands of Flores and Timor in the Eastern Indonesian Archipelago and establish a seminary on the island of Solor, off the eastern tip of Flores. [**Asia: Indonesia, Timor-Leste**]

1596 The first Dutch Protestants arrive in Malacca, challenging the dominance of the Portuguese Catholics in the Malaysian peninsula, gradually gaining control of the spice trade in the Moluccas, and capturing Malacca in 1641. [**Asia: Malaysia**]

1596 The Union of Brest-Litovsk creates the Ukrainian Greek Catholic Church, reuniting both the Roman Catholic (Polish) and the Orthodox (Ukrainian) factions into an Orthodox Ukrainian church in union with Rome (i.e. "the Uniates"). [**Europe: Ukraine**]

1597 Rivalry between the Portuguese Jesuits and the Spanish Dominicans leads to a wave of persecution and mass executions of Christians in Japan, beginning with the crucifixion of the crew of the stranded Spanish ship *San Felipe*. [**Asia: Japan**]

1598 Hideyoshi's death brings an end to the persecution of the Christians, and Jesuit, Franciscan, and Dominican missions continue in Japan. [**Asia: Japan**]

1598 King Henry IV of France issues the Edict of Nantes granting freedom of worship to the French Calvinist Protestants (Huguenots); however, this Edict would be revoked by King Louis XIV in 1685. [**Europe: France**]

1599 Peruvian Amerindian Martin de Porres becomes a lay Dominican Friar in Lima and famous for his holiness and care of the sick (including the working of miracles); he dies in 1639 and is canonized in 1962. [**Latin America and the Caribbean: Peru**]

1599 Portuguese archbishop Alexis de Menezes of Goa calls the Synod of Udiyamperur (Diamper) to bring the Malabar church under Latin control; as part of this, the Synod orders that the church's Syriac manuscripts, books, and relics are to be examined and, if in grievous error, burnt. [**Asia: India**]

1600 Matteo Ricci finally reaches Peking, where he offers gifts (including a clock and a harpsichord) to the Emperor and becomes close to many in the Imperial Court; by the time of his death in 1610, there are two thousand five hundred Christians in the Court. [**Asia: China**]

A Timeline of Global Christianity

1600 The victory of the daimyo (feudal baron) Tokugawa Ieyasu in the Battle of Sekigahara brings about the reunification of Japan and the establishment of the Tokugawa Shōgunate (military dictatorship), which would govern Japan until 1868. [**Asia: Japan**]

1601 After working for seventeen years among the Igorot headhunter gold-mining forest tribes of Luzon, the Augustinian missionary Esteban Marin dies as a martyr while attempting to pacify mountain settlements in eastern Pampanga during a Spanish expedition to subdue an Igorot revolt. [**Asia: Philippines**]

1601 The Jesuits ordain their first Japanese priests during a twelve-year period of toleration (1601–1613) following Tokugawa Ieyasu's seizure of power the previous year. [**Asia: Japan**]

1603 Matteo Ricci publishes his book *Tianzhu shi yi* (*The True Meaning of the Lord of Heaven*), a presentation of Christianity in Chinese philosophical (i.e. Confucian) categories; this book receives a warm reception from Chinese scholars. [**Asia: China**]

1603 The moral influence of Matteo Ricci and his fellow Jesuit missionaries leads to the conversion of Xu Guangshi, the first of the Three Pillars (three upper-class scholar-officials who become highly influential in building Chinese Catholicism). [**Asia: China**]

1604 King James I convenes the Hampton Court Conference with representatives of the Church of England (including the Puritans); this leads to the translation and publication of the Authorized Version of the Bible (also known as the King James Bible) in 1611, which exerts a formative influence on English language and religion. [**Europe: United Kingdom of Great Britain and Northern Ireland (England)**]

1604 The Jesuit mission in Cabo Verde begins, partly through the urging of Balthasar Barreira, a Portuguese-African layman who had previously worked with the Jesuits for thirteen years in Angola. [**Africa: Cabo Verde**]

1604–1605 French colonists establish a settlement at Île-Saint Croix in Passamaquoddy Bay; after almost perishing due to the lack of resources during the winter months, the settlement relocates across the Bay of Fundy to Port Royal in Nova Scotia, where British invasion forces finally destroy it in 1613. [**North America: Canada**]

1605 The Dutch seize the island of Amboina (Ambon) in the Moluccas, beginning two centuries of Dutch hegemony throughout the East Indies and establishing the dominance of Protestant Christianity in the Moluccas. [**Asia: Indonesia**]

1605 The Jesuit missionary Robert de Nobili, the pioneer in using cultural accommodation (the adaptation of those local customs and practices that do not counteract Christianity) in missionary work, arrives in India. [**Asia: India**]

1607 English Anglicans under the leadership of Captain Edward Maria Wingfield set up the first settler colonies at Jamestown in Virginia with the intention of reproducing the Church of England across the Atlantic. [**North America: United States of America**]

1608 French explorer Samuel de Champlain founds the Catholic settler city of Quebec near the mouth of the St. Lawrence River and begins to consolidate the colonies of "New France" in continental North America; the Jesuits begin missionary work here three years later. [**North America: Canada**]

1609 The Spanish Crown gives the Jesuits control of Paraguay and of large parts of inland South America, leading to the formation of a creative network of thirty mission colonies or "Reductions" (from Spanish *reducciónes*) for the Guaraní Indians. [**Latin America and the Caribbean: Argentina, Brazil, Paraguay, Plurinational State of Bolivia, Uruguay**]

1610 Italian astronomer Galileo Galilei discovers the moons of Jupiter, thereby confirming Copernicus's theory of planetary movements around the sun. [**Europe: Italy**]

1614 Under the shōgun Tokugawa Ieyasu, an intense persecution begins in response to the rising power of the Christian daimyos; this leads to the closure of churches, the expulsion of missionaries, the torture and martyrdom of Christians, and the eventual prohibition of Christianity. [**Asia: Japan**]

1615 Incan convert Felipe Guáman Poma de Ayala sends a handwritten illustrated manuscript to King Philip III of Spain, describing the Indians' plight under the conquistadores and calling for greater justice. [**Latin America and the Caribbean: Peru**]

A Timeline of Global Christianity

1616 Tokugawa Ieyasu intensifies the persecution of Christians, seeking out and imprisoning any remaining missionaries (especially in Nagasaki), eventually burning them alive, and beheading all local Christians. [**Asia: Japan**]

1618 The Protestant citizens of Prague throw the Holy Roman Emperor's regents from the windows of the council room in Hradčany Castle; although they are not injured, this act of rebellion, known as the "Defenestration of Prague," leads to the outbreak of the Thirty Years' War (1618–1648), the last war of religion in Europe. [**Europe: Czechia (Czech Republic)**]

1618 The Synod of Dort articulates the Calvinist Reformed Faith in the Canons of Dort in an attempt to resolve the Arminian controversy of that day in the light of John Calvin's teaching; these canons have since become a key confessional standard of many Reformed Churches worldwide. [**Europe: Netherlands**]

1620 French philosopher Rene Descartes postulates the idea of skeptical rationality in his dictum "Cogito, ergo sum" (I doubt, therefore I exist). [**Europe: Germany**]

1620 The Mayflower Pilgrim Fathers (led by a party of Independent Separatists, who had previously sought freedom from religious persecution in Leyden in the Netherlands) land at Plymouth Rock, thereby beginning the settlement of Puritan and Separatist colonies in New England. [**North America: United States of America**]

1621 Augustinian archbishop Miguel Garcia Serrano of Manila ordains Augustin Tabuyo as the first Filipino priest. [**Asia: Philippines**]

1622 Persecution in Nagasaki reaches a peak under the second shōgun Tokugawa Hidetada; over the next seventeen years, thousands of Christians are killed or mercilessly tortured to renounce their faith, resulting in the almost total extinction of Christianity in Japan until the nineteenth century. [**Asia: Japan**]

1622 Pope Gregory XV creates the Congregatio de Propaganda Fide (Congregation for the Propagation of the Faith), a new, centralized body in Rome to oversee the theory and practice of Catholic missions throughout the world. [**Europe: Italy**]

1622 The Ethiopian Emperor Susneyos converts to Catholicism through the influence of the Spanish Jesuit missionary Pedro Paez. [**Africa: Ethiopia**]

1623 Jesuit missionaries in China discover the Xi'an-fu monument, set up in 781 and telling the story of the arrival and progress of Christianity in China from 635 on. [**Asia: China**]

1624 The French Jesuit Alexandre de Rhodes arrives in Viet Nam and becomes the key figure in Catholic mission in Southeast Asia, setting up churches with local, rather than European, clergy. [**Asia: Viet Nam**]

1624 The Jesuit Antonio de Andrade briefly visits Tibet, returning two years later at the invitation of the Buddhist ruler of Tsaparang and opening the first (although short lived) Christian church there. [**Asia: (Tibet)**]

1625 After having been driven out of Acadia (Nova Scotia) by a British invasion in 1613, the Jesuits return to Quebec to resume missionary work. [**North America: Canada**]

1626 Dutch colonists land in Taiwan, with the first ordained missionary-chaplain, Georgius Candidius, arriving the following year. [**Asia: (Taiwan)**]

1626 The Dutch East India Company founds a colony on Manhattan Island on the Hudson River, naming it New Amsterdam; the appointment of a Dutch Reformed minister to the colony two years later introduces Presbyterian models of church polity to the American colonies. [**North America: United States of America**]

1628 Puritan settlers, driven from England by the repressive measures of King Charles I because of their attempts to reform the Church of England from within, establish the first Puritan colonies in Massachusetts Bay. [**North America: United States of America**]

1629 Albert Cornelius Ruyl, a Dutch East Indies trader, makes the first translation of a part of the Bible into a non-European language in the modern period, the Gospel of Matthew into Bahasa Melayu (the "High" form of the Malay language); his translation also contained a selection of other Bible portions (such as the Ten Commandments and the Lord's Prayer) for catechetical and liturgical use. [**Asia: Malaysia**]

A Timeline of Global Christianity

1632 The Emperor Susneyos abdicates in favor of his non-Catholic son Fasildas to end hardline Catholic demands and to avoid a civil war; this leads to the expulsion of the Jesuits and other Catholic missionaries, two centuries of closure to all Europeans, and an enduring heritage of distrust. [**Africa: Ethiopia**]

1634 Cecilius Calvert, the second Lord Baltimore, inherits a grant of American land which had been made to his father by the British Crown in 1632, and sets it up as the Catholic settlement of Maryland, a colony where Catholics could live in peace. [**North America: United States of America**]

1636 After being expelled from the colony of Massachusetts for spreading "new and dangerous ideas," radical Independent Roger Williams sets up the colony of Providence Plantation (later Rhode Island) as a refuge for religious minorities; he later founds the First Baptist Church of Providence, the first Baptist church in America. [**North America: United States of America**]

1636 Despite the initial Jesuit policy of cultural accommodation in the Chinese mission, the Rites Controversy (a dispute over the religious nature of Chinese rituals) begins, leading to two centuries of deep division between the Chinese church, the papacy, and the Chinese State. [**Asia: China**]

1637 The Shimabara Rebellion (the "Farmers' Revolt") of peasants and Catholic Christians breaks out against the Tokugawa Shōgunate in response to drastically increased taxes and to religious persecution. [**Asia: Japan**]

1639 A small party of Ursuline Nuns, led by Marie de l'Incarnation, enters New France, establishing a convent in Quebec, and founding the first school for girls in North America. [**North America: Canada**]

1639 After a quarter of a century of intense persecution, Christianity becomes almost completely extinct in Japan, with only a few small hidden communities remaining; all links with the West are closed except for a small Dutch enclave on an offshore island (Dejima or "Exit Island"). [**Asia: Japan**]

1641 The King of Portugal bars the access of his subjects to the Jesuit settlements in La Guayra in order to protect their Indian inhabitants from the depredations of colonists and from bands of Portuguese-Indian half-castes who are carrying them away into slavery. [**Latin America and the Caribbean: Paraguay**]

1641–1646 The English Civil War breaks out between High Church Royalists (the "Cavaliers") and Puritan Parliamentarians (the "Roundheads"); the latter party's victory ends the Church of England's religious monopoly. [**Europe: United Kingdom of Great Britain and Northern Ireland (England)**]

1642 Jesuit Jean de Leria attempts the first Christian mission to Laos, staying for five years before pressure from Buddhist monks forces him to leave the country. [**Asia: Lao People's Democratic Republic**]

1643–1649 The Westminster Assembly meets to consolidate English Reformed orthodoxy, enshrining this in the Westminster Confession of Faith, a systematic exposition of Calvinist orthodoxy and Puritan theology. [**Europe: United Kingdom of Great Britain and Northern Ireland (England)**]

1644 The French Capuchins start a mission in Whydah, but are later expelled by English and Dutch slave traders; the area becomes (with neighboring Togo), the center of the slave export trade in the 1670s and known as "the Slave Coast." [**Africa: Benin, Togo**]

1645 Pope Innocent X creates a Prefecture Apostolic for Kongo and puts this in the hands of the Italian Capuchins (a strict Franciscan rule). [**Africa: Angola, Congo, Democratic Republic of the Congo**]

1647 George Fox experiences the first of his "openings" (or illuminations of inner light) and begins to preach; this results in the formation of the Quakers, later called the Society of Friends. [**Europe: United Kingdom of Great Britain and Northern Ireland (England)**]

1648 The signing of the series of peace treaties known as the Peace of Westphalia ends the Thirty Years' War, resulting in a radically changed balance of power and the emergence of modern Europe as a community of sovereign states. [**Europe: Germany**]

1649 As part of a campaign of genocide, Iroquois raiding parties attack the Hurons at St. Ignace in New France, destroying the Jesuit mission there, and savagely torturing missionaries Jean de Brébeuf, Gabriel Lalemant, Antoine Daniel, Charles Garnier, and Noel Charbanel to death. [**North America: Canada**]

A Timeline of Global Christianity

1649 Following the end of the second phase of the English Civil War and the trial and execution of King Charles I, England becomes a republican Commonwealth ruled by the Rump Parliament and a Council of State; this Parliament is dissolved four years later and Oliver Cromwell becomes Lord Protector of the English Commonwealth until the Restoration of the Monarchy under King Charles II in 1660. [**Europe: United Kingdom of Great Britain and Northern Ireland (England)**]

1652 The Dutch establish a settlement at the Cape of Good Hope to safeguard their trade routes to India and the East Indies; this settlement has significance for Christian mission only to the extent that the Khoikhoi local people became "Dutchified," adopting Dutch ways of living, including their Protestant religion. [**Africa: South Africa**]

1652 The Jesuit orator, writer, and missionary Antonio Vieira argues for the removal of the Indians of Brazil from the jurisdiction of the Portuguese colonial governors in order to prevent their exploitation. [**Latin America and the Caribbean: Brazil**]

1652 Tsar Alexis I appoints Nikon as Patriarch of the Russian Church; as Patriarch, Nikon controversially attempts to restore the church to a Greek Orthodox model, leading to schism between the traditionalist "Old Believers" and the main body of the Russian Church. [**Europe: Russian Federation**]

1653 The Coonen Cross revolt breaks out between the Syrian Thomas Christians (who seek the expulsion of the Jesuits from India) and the Catholic authorities; this results in the separation of the Malabar and Catholic Churches for centuries. [**Asia: India**]

1655–1709 After a number of sporadic and largely unsuccessful attempts to establish a Christian presence in Thailand in 1567–1569, 1606–1609, and 1626–1632, a permanent Jesuit mission finally begins under Thomas Valguarnera. [**Asia: Thailand**]

1656 In Manila, the Dominicans ordain Luo Wenzao (also known as Gregory López) as their first Chinese priest; he later receives consecration in China in 1685 as bishop, becoming the only Chinese Catholic bishop until 1926. [**Asia: China**]

1658 The Dutch Reformed missionary Philip Baldeus arrives in northern Sri Lanka and establishes a number of Reformed Christian communities in the Jaffna area. [**Asia: Sri Lanka**]

1660 The failure of the Puritan republic after Oliver Cromwell's death in 1658 leads to the Restoration of the Monarchy and the crowning of King Charles II as monarch of England, Scotland, and Ireland; although Charles favors a policy of religious tolerance, the reinstatement of the Anglican Church as the established Church of England follows his accession to the throne. [**Europe: United Kingdom of Great Britain and Northern Ireland (England)**]

1662 The expulsion of the Dutch by the Chinese buccaneer Koxinga (Cheng Ch'eng-Kung) and the subsequent anti-Christian persecution of the Christian tribal communities lead to the disappearance of Christianity in Taiwan. [**Asia: (Taiwan)**]

1662 The introduction of the "Halfway Covenant" (whereby baptized children of godly parents are recognized as being part of the Church, even though they themselves had not professed faith) in Massachusetts indicates that the Puritan ideal of a godly society had not been fully realized in the colony. [**North America: United States of America**]

1664 The Apostolic Vicar Pierre Lambert de la Motte, together with several newly arrived French bishops and nine indigenous priests, convenes the Tonkin Synod in Ayutthia to plan a Catholic missionary strategy for all of Asia. [**Asia: Thailand, Viet Nam**]

1665 The Angolan invasion of Kongo weakens Kongolese Christianity, leading to the later emergence of several women prophets, the most significant of these being Dona Beatriz Kimpa Vita. [**Africa: Angola, Congo, Democratic Republic of the Congo**]

1668 Spanish explorer Diego Luis de Sanvitores leads a Jesuit mission into the Pacific; although the mission has some initial success, it is also characterized by brutality and repression, and after twenty-three years of resistance to this, only five thousand of the indigenous Chamorro population of one hundred thousand had survived, due to Spanish colonial genocide and to their introduction of new diseases. [**Oceania: Federated States of Micronesia, Guam, Northern Mariana Islands**]

1671 Pope Clement X canonizes the ascetic Dominican lay tertiary Isabel Flores de Oliva (known as "Saint Rose of Lima") fifty-four years after her death in 1617 at the age of thirty-one; as the first American-born saint, she is venerated as the patron saint of Peru, all of South

America, the West Indies, and the Philippines. [**Latin America and the Caribbean: Peru**]

1673 The English Parliament passes the Test Act, limiting access to public office and education to practicing Anglicans in communion with the Church of England, and excluding Catholics and other nonconformists; this Act remains in force until 1829. [**Europe: United Kingdom of Great Britain and Northern Ireland (England)**]

1675 Philipp Jakob Spener publishes his book *Pia Desideria* (*Pious Desires*), in which he seeks to reform the lifestyle of the Lutheran church by cultivating a personal, warmhearted relationship with Christ; this lays the foundations of the influential Pietist movement. [**Europe: Germany**]

1681–1682 Quaker land entrepreneur William Penn founds the Province of Pennsylvania on the basis of religious tolerance, renouncing the use of coercion and granting free exercise of religion to all, which draws many persecuted minorities to settle there; this religious tolerance is later incorporated into the Pennsylvania Charter of Privileges in 1701. [**North America: United States of America**]

1682 The French Catholic (Gallican) Church issues the Four Articles, a declaration of their position vis-à-vis papal authority; these are condemned by Pope Alexander VIII in 1690. [**Europe: France**]

1685 King Louis XIV issues the Edict of Fontainebleu, revoking the 1598 Edict of Nantes, thus making Protestantism illegal in France and providing the catalyst for an exodus of French Calvinist Protestants (Huguenots) to the Netherlands and England. [**Europe: France**]

1686 Black Catholic Lourenço da Silva de Mendouça (who, although a layman, claims descent from the kings of Kongo and Angola) petitions the Vatican against perpetual slavery and the cruelty that accompanies it. [**Africa: Angola**]

1687 Following a powerful 8.4–8.7 magnitude *terremoto* (earthquake) which devastates Lima and other parts of Peru and kills more than five thousand people, the Jesuits introduce the Three Hour Service, a prayerful meditation on Jesus's last seven words from the Cross, into Catholic liturgies for Good Friday. [**Latin America and the Caribbean: Peru**]

1688 The Dutch Protestant Prince William of Orange invades England and, with influential English political and religious support, deposes the Catholic King James II and accedes to the English throne. [**Europe: United Kingdom of Great Britain and Northern Ireland (England)**]

1692 An outbreak of mass hysteria in colonial Massachusetts culminates in the Salem Witch Trials and in the execution of about twenty people, almost all of whom are women, for witchcraft. [**North America: United States of America**]

1693 Charles Maigrot, the feisty Vicar Apostolic of Fujian, orders Chinese rites such as the veneration of ancestors to be discontinued; Pope Clement XI enforces and extends this ban eleven years later. [**Asia: China**]

1694 August Hermann Francke takes up the chair of Greek and oriental languages in the newly reorganized University of Halle and extends the influence of Philipp Jakob Spener's Pietism, emphasizing the inner life of the individual (the "religion of the warm heart"). [**Europe: Germany**]

1695 English philosopher John Locke publishes his book *The Reasonableness of Christianity*, in which he insists that the beliefs of Christianity are rational, and that every individual has the ability and responsibility to achieve salvation by means of the Scriptures; his emphasis on individual responsibility provides a foundation for religious toleration and freedom of conscience, and helps to lay the foundations of Deism and Liberalism. [**Europe: United Kingdom of Great Britain and Northern Ireland (England)**]

1696 Irish rationalist philosopher John Toland argues in his *Christianity not Mysterious* that "there is nothing in the Gospel contrary to reason, nor above it" and that there is therefore no need for revelation in religion; in his view, Christianity is essentially a reiteration of the religion of nature. [**Europe: Ireland**]

1698 Anglican priest Thomas Bray, together with some influential friends, founds the Society for Promoting Christian Knowledge (SPCK) to promote Christian education and the distribution of Christian literature; they also set up a related Church of England missionary organization, the Society for the Propagation of the Gospel in Foreign Parts

(SPG), three years later. [**Europe: United Kingdom of Great Britain and Northern Ireland (England)**]

1700s Both the Kongo nation and the Kongo church begin a long period of decline that would extend throughout the eighteenth century. [**Africa: Angola, Congo, Democratic Republic of the Congo**]

1701 The newly founded Anglican SPG begins its activities in America, particularly in the lower South, the mid-Atlantic colonies, and New England, as well as in Bermuda and in those colonies that would later become part of Canada. [**North America: Bermuda, Canada, United States of America**]

1703 French Catholic trainee priest Claude-François Poullart des Places founds a Catholic educational and mission group, the Holy Ghost Fathers (or "Spiritans") in Paris; after being reconstituted in 1848, this group would have major influence on nineteenth-century Catholic mission, especially in Africa. [**Europe: France**]

1706 Two German Pietist Lutheran clerics, Bartholomaeus Ziegenbalg and Heinrich Plutschau, arrive in the Danish colony of Tranquebar to begin the first Protestant missionary work to the Indians (the Danish-Halle Mission). [**Asia: India**]

1710–1711 Two Franciscan friars, Carlo Maria de Genova and Severino da Silesia, cross the Sahara from Tripoli to make contact with Christians reported to be among the Kwararafa people, but die of sickness in Katsina, Northern Nigeria. [**Africa: Libya, Niger, Nigeria**]

1712 Governor Christopher Codrington bequeaths his two Barbados estates to the Anglican SPG as the foundation of a College. [**Latin America and the Caribbean: Barbados**]

1716 After a journey of ten months from Srinagar via Kashmir and Ladakh, the Italian Jesuit missionary Ippolito (Hippolyte) Desideri reaches Lhasa, where he attempts to revive Christian work in Tibet; however, he leaves five years later without having found any evidence of a surviving Christian community there. [**Asia: (Tibet)**]

1721 As part of his program of the reform and Westernization of all aspects of Russian life, Tsar Peter the Great abolishes the Moscow patriarchate and puts the Russian Orthodox Church under the jurisdiction of a government-controlled "Most Holy Governing Synod." [**Europe: Russian Federation**]

1722 Count Nicholas von Zinzendorf sets up a Pietist Moravian community on his estate of Herrnhut in Saxony; this community experiences an outpouring of the Spirit in 1727, leading to the emergence of the Moravians as a major missionary movement. [**Europe: Germany**]

1724 Roman Catholic intransigence on the Rites Controversy offends the Chinese government and the Emperor Yung Cheng consequently outlaws Christianity (although this edict mainly affects foreigners, rather than Chinese Christians). [**Asia: China**]

1734–1743 The "Great Awakening" begins under Theodore Frelinghuysen, Gilbert Tennent, and (especially) Jonathan Edwards; the preaching of George Whitefield and others reinforces its impact after 1740. [**North America: United States of America**]

1738 German Moravian missionary Georg Schmidt builds a farm at Genadendal (Valley of Grace) near Cape Town and preaches to his Khoikhoi farm hands, baptizing some of them; despite this success, the Dutch Reformed Church in the Netherlands expels him as a heretic in 1744, claiming that he had been improperly ordained and that only Dutch Reformed ministers had the authority to baptize. [**Africa: South Africa**]

1738 Moravian influence leads Anglican clergyman John Wesley to his "heartwarming" conversion at Aldersgate Street in London; Wesley begins field-preaching (i.e. preaching in the open air) to the poor the following year, thus launching the Methodist movement. [**Europe: United Kingdom of Great Britain and Northern Ireland (England)**]

1740 Italian Cardinal Prospero Lorenzo Lambertini of the Basilica of the Holy Cross in Jerusalem becomes Benedict XIV, the great pope of the eighteenth century. [**Europe: Italy**]

1742 Former Ghanaian slave Jacobus Capitein presents his doctoral dissertation to Leiden University, defending the slave trade as compatible with Christianity; he later becomes a Dutch Reformed minister in Ghana. [**Africa: Ghana**]

1742 Pope Benedict XIV issues the papal bull *Ex quo singulari*, stating that Chinese rites such as the veneration of ancestors are unacceptable; this authoritative ruling adds to Chinese misgivings about Catholic missionaries. [**Asia: China**]

A Timeline of Global Christianity

1742 The Nubian servant of a Franciscan friar in Cairo reports that a single isolated Christian community still exists, despite persecution, in the Third Cataract region of Nubia. [**Africa: Sudan**]

1749 Enlightenment thinker and moderate Deist Benjamin Franklin urges the development of a "Publick Religion," which, although rejecting organized forms of religion, would nevertheless foster moral virtue along the lines of Christianity. [**North America: United States of America**]

1750 German Pietist missionary Christian Friedrich Schwartz arrives in Tranquebar on the Tamil Nadu coast; after fifteen years there, he begins ministry in the British garrison of Trichinopoly, 150 kilometers further inland, where he wins many Indian converts, becoming famous throughout Southern India over the next thirty years. [**Asia: India**]

1752 The Anglican SPG sends its first missionary, Thomas Thompson, to the Cape Coast (Ghana), where he concentrates on ministry to the local people, rather than on a chaplaincy to the expatriate enclaves. [**Africa: Ghana**]

1757 British troops under Robert Clive defeat the French at the Battle of Plassey and this victory, together with the collapse of the Mughal Empire in 1761, opens the way for the mercantile and political dominance of the British East India Company and eventually the establishment of the British Raj (the rule of the British Crown in the Indian subcontinent) one hundred years later. [**Asia: India**]

1763 The British conquest of "New France" (1756–1760) forces France to cede all of Canada at the Treaty of Paris; however, Roman Catholics are guaranteed the free exercise of their religion, enabling old-school French churchmen to maintain the national Catholic culture, especially in Quebec. [**North America: Canada**]

1765 After being taken to England as a child for his education by an Anglican SPG missionary, Fante Christian Philip Quaque studies theology and becomes the first ordained African priest in the Church of England; as such, he succeeds Thomas Thompson as chaplain at Cape Coast Castle (a transfer station for the slave trade) in 1766, and works there for the next fifty years. [**Africa: Ghana**]

1765–1783 The American Revolution begins, in which the American Colonies reject British taxation and authority; this Revolution leads to the War of Independence (1775–1783), the ratifying of the Declaration of Independence (1776), and the foundation of the United States of America. **[North America: United States of America]**

1766 Three years before Captain Cook's arrival in New Zealand in 1769, the Māori *tohunga matakite* (priestly seer) Arama Te Toiroa prophesies the coming of the pākehā (white men) in sailing ships, predicting that "*Te ingoa o tō rātou Atua, ko Tama-i-rorokutia, he Atua pai, otirā, ka ngaro āno te tāngata.* [The name of their God will be Tama-i-rorokutia—the Son who was killed—a good god; however the people will still be oppressed.]" **[Oceania: New Zealand]**

1768 As part of the Bourbon Reforms in Spain and its territories, the Spanish King Carlos III (with support from influential parties within the Spanish church) expels the Jesuit order from the Philippines in order to curb colonial autonomy and to assert royal control. **[Asia: Philippines]**

1769 English explorer Captain James Cook arrives in Tahiti on the first of his three expeditions in the Pacific; his instructions on this first voyage are to observe and record the transit of Venus on June 3 from Tahiti and thereafter to search the South Pacific for the postulated southern continent of Terra Australis Incognita (Unknown Southern Land). **[Oceania: French Polynesia]**

1772 French-born Philadelphia Quaker and abolitionist Anthony Benezet publishes his pamphlet *Some historical account of Guinea* attacking the slave trade and the institution of slavery; he also founds one of the first antislavery societies, the Society for the Relief of Free Negroes Unlawfully Held in Bondage in 1775. **[Africa: Guinea]**

1773 After the suppression of the Jesuits in many European countries and overseas dominions because of their reputation for political maneuvering and economic power, Pope Clement XIV issues the bull *Dominus ac Redemptor noster* dissolving the order; this leads to a decline in Catholic missions worldwide. **[Europe: Italy]**

1777 The Moravians establish a mission in the Danish colony of Serampore, but abandon this in 1792, on the eve of William Carey's arrival in

India, because of the lack of cooperation from their fellow German Pietists. [**Asia: India**]

1781 English Anglican Robert Raikes, editor of the *Gloucester Journal*, publicizes the formation of Sunday Schools in Gloucestershire and elsewhere, and starts a similar school for the education of the children of factory workers and farm laborers using the Bible as a textbook; this marks the beginning of the Sunday School movement. [**Europe: United Kingdom of Great Britain and Northern Ireland (England)**]

1783 Korean scholar Lee Seung-Hun (also known as Yi Seung-Hun) visits Beijing, where Jean-Joseph de Grammont, a former Jesuit missionary, baptizes him; this introduces Catholic Christianity into Korea, despite the initial absence of priests. [**Asia: Republic of Korea (South Korea)**]

1784 The British Parliament passes Prime Minister William Pitt the Younger's India Act, by which all activities of the British East India Company come under the control of the British government, represented in India by the Governor-General. [**Asia: India**]

1786 The General Assembly of Virginia passes Thomas Jefferson's bill guaranteeing religious liberty for all; this forms the basis of the First Amendment to the American Constitution in 1791: "Congress shall make no law respecting an establishment of religion, or prohibiting the free exercise thereof. . . ." [**North America: United States of America**]

1787 The British Crown founds a settlement in Sierra Leone for freed slaves and the dregs of London society, but this is not initially successful as a local chieftain burns it to the ground two years later, necessitating its rebuilding in 1791. [**Africa: Sierra Leone**]

1787 The Fante abolitionist Ottobah Cugoano publishes his *Thoughts and sentiments on the evil and wicked traffic of the slavery and commerce of the human species, humbly submitted to the inhabitants of Great-Britain*, calling for the abolition of slavery and the immediate emancipation of all slaves. [**Africa: Ghana**]

1788 The "First Fleet" of eleven ships arrives in Botany Bay to found a penal colony for convicts sentenced to transportation to Australia; more than one hundred sixty-six thousand convicts are transported under this policy until its abolition in 1868. [**Oceania: Australia**]

1789 Vicar Apostolic Pigneau de Behaine secures the restoration of the exiled ruler of Cochin China, Nguyễn Ánh, who adopts the dynastic name of Gia Long (a combination of elements of the Vietnamese names for Saigon and Hanoi) to symbolize the unification of northern and southern Viet Nam under his rule. [**Asia: Viet Nam**]

1789 The French Revolution begins with the storming of the Bastille (a medieval fortress, armory, and political prison in Paris); the Bastille symbolizes royal authority, and hence the abuses of the monarchy. [**Europe: France**]

1789 Well-known freed Igbo slave Olaudah Equiano (also known as Gustavus Vassa) publishes his book *The interesting narrative of the life of Olaudah Equiano, or Gustavus Vassa, the African*, an articulate, intelligent, English-speaking African voice against slavery. [**Africa: Nigeria**]

1789–1790 Korean Christian Lee Seung-Hun writes letters to the Catholic missionaries in Beijing asking for their help for the nascent, but persecuted, church that had grown from his enthusiastic evangelism on his return to Korea after his baptism in Beijing. [**Asia: Republic of Korea (South Korea)**]

1792 A party of Nova Scotians (i.e. black Canadians whose ancestors had fled the colonial United States as slaves or freemen) arrives in Sierra Leone, with Bibles in hand and singing hymns; their arrival represents a refounding of the Sierra Leone settlement. [**Africa: Sierra Leone**]

1792 Moravian missionaries return to South Africa and find that the converts of the pioneer missionary Georg Schmidt had not only survived despite official opposition, but also continued to meet under the same tree where he had taught them to read the Bible and pray fifty-five years earlier. [**Africa: South Africa**]

1792 William Carey publishes his landmark book *An Enquiry into the Obligation of Christians to Use Means for the Conversion of the Heathens, in which the Religious State of the Different Nations of the World, the Success of Former Undertakings, and the Practicability of Further Undertakings Are Considered* and, with several others, forms the English Baptist Missionary Society, effectively beginning the modern foreign mission movement in the English-speaking Protestant world.

[Europe: United Kingdom of Great Britain and Northern Ireland (England)]

1793 The ascetic monastic and miracle-worker Seraphim of Sarov, the most famous of the Russian startsy (elders), retires to a log cabin in the forests outside Sarov, where he remains for the next twenty-five years as a solitary hermit. [**Europe: Russian Federation**]

1793 The Italian explorer Alejandro Malaspina's crew, which includes two priests, probably celebrates mass on board ship while anchored in Doubtful Sound, making this the first Christian service in New Zealand. [**Oceania: New Zealand**]

1793 William Carey begins his missionary work in India, producing (together with his team of native-speaking Indians) the first draft in Bengali of the entire New Testament, and also of parts of the Old Testament only three years later. [**Asia: India**]

1794 Anglican clergyman Samuel Marsden arrives in Parramatta as the chaplain to the convict colony in Sydney and makes several unsuccessful attempts to civilize and evangelize the Aboriginals. [**Oceania: Australia**]

1795–1804 The formation of a number of voluntarist evangelical and missionary societies enlarges the constituency of the Protestant missionary movement; these significant new groups include the Congregationalist London Missionary Society (LMS) in 1795; the Nederlandsch Zendelinggenootschap (Netherlands Missionary Society, NZG) in 1797; the Evangelical Anglican Church Missionary Society (CMS) in 1799; and the British and Foreign Bible Society in 1804. [**Europe: Netherlands, United Kingdom of Great Britain and Northern Ireland (England)**]

1796 The nondenominational LMS sends the ship *Duff* on the first Protestant mission to the Pacific; in March 1797 it arrives in Matavai Bay on the north coast of Tahiti, the location of Captain Cook's observations of the transit of Venus in 1769. [**Oceania: French Polynesia**]

1797 The LMS sends a party of ten missionaries to Tonga but fails in its first attempts to establish Christianity there, with three missionaries being killed in a tribal war, another defecting from the mission, and the remainder evacuating to Sydney. [**Oceania: Tonga**]

1797 Samuel Marsden develops an interest in mission after the arrival of the Tongan LMS missionaries in Sydney and takes up the supervision of the CMS's affairs; Sydney becomes the CMS base in the Southwestern Pacific. [**Oceania: Australia**]

1799 German theologian Friedrich Schleiermacher publishes his influential *Über die Religion: Reden an die Gebildeten unter ihren Verächtern* (*On Religion: Speeches to Its Cultured Despisers*) appealing to the role of feeling in Christian faith and focusing on the nature of religious experience. [**Europe: Germany**]

1799 The Dutch LMS missionary Johannes van der Kemp arrives in Cape Town to begin missionary work, initially among the Xhosa, but later among the Khoikhoi. [**Africa: South Africa**]

1800 The Confucianist Emperor Jiaqing, faced with growing rebellion against his rule in China, issues a Discourse on Heretical Religions and launches a major attempt to wipe out these religions (including Christianity), by "scouring with sand" (the Chinese term for torture and obliteration). [**Asia: China**]

1801 A major persecution of Catholics in Korea breaks out, with Lee Seung-Hun, pioneer priest James Chou Wen-mo and more than three hundred Christians being killed. [**Asia: Republic of Korea (South Korea)**]

1801 After beginning in the late 1790s, the revival known as the "Second Great Awakening" gains momentum and spreads in all directions from a series of camp meetings at Cane Ridge, Kentucky, especially amongst Baptist and Methodist frontier communities. [**North America: United States of America**]

1801 Congregationalists in New England and Presbyterians in the United States adopt a "Plan of Union" uniting the two churches; however, controversy over the Congregationalist "New England theology" leads to the "Old School" Presbyterian Church ending cooperation with them in 1837, and the Union with the remaining "New School" Presbyterians breaking up fifteen years later. [**North America: United States of America**]

1802–1820 The tolerant regime of Emperor Gia Long brings a period of freedom and growth for the Christian church in Viet Nam, but vicious persecution breaks out after his death. [**Asia: Viet Nam**]

A Timeline of Global Christianity

1805 The "Serampore Trio" of William Carey, Joshua Marshman, and William Ward outline a ten-point form of organization for future missionary endeavors; this "Serampore Covenant" sets the Protestant pattern for Christian expansion in Asia for the next century. [**Asia: India**]

1806 Anglican priest and missionary Henry Martyn arrives in India as a chaplain to the East India Company; although he only works for six years in India (dying in 1812) he is highly effective as a linguist, translating the New Testament into Hindustani, Urdu, and Persian. [**Asia: India**]

1806 The British set up the Cape Colony at the Cape of Good Hope, superseding the Dutch, who had maintained a colony there for much of the previous 150 years; Protestant missions in southern Africa begin in earnest from this new starting point. [**Africa: South Africa**]

1807 As a result of more than twenty years of tireless effort by Evangelical English parliamentarian William Wilberforce and other abolitionists, Parliament passes the Slave Trade Act, making the slave trade illegal in Britain, although slavery itself is not finally abolished until 1833. [**Europe: United Kingdom of Great Britain and Northern Ireland (England)**]

1807 Following its banning of the slave trade, the British Parliament sends a naval squadron to patrol the West Coast of Africa, intercept transatlantic slave ships, and repatriate the freed slaves to Sierra Leone. [**Africa: Sierra Leone**]

1807 Robert Morrison arrives in Guangzhou (Canton) under the auspices of the LMS as part of the first Protestant mission to enter China. [**Asia: China**]

1810 Recent graduates of Williams College (where the famous 1806 "Haystack Prayer Meeting" had taken place, birthing the American Foreign Mission movement) establish the American Board of Commissioners for Foreign Missions (ABCFM) to facilitate missionary work. [**North America: United States of America**]

1810 The Argentine War of Independence begins, the first in a series of Latin American political revolutions leading to the liberation of almost all South American countries from colonial (mostly Spanish) rule by 1831; the Vatican, however, sides with the Spanish Crown. **[Latin America and the Caribbean: Argentina]**

1810 The Catholic priest Miguel Hidalgo y Costilla proclaims the Grito de Dolores (Cry of Dolores), marking the beginning of the Mexican War of Independence, and ultimately leading to Mexico's liberation from Spain in 1821. **[Latin America and the Caribbean: Mexico]**

1810 The Dutch LMS missionary Johannes van der Kemp proposes the holding of a world missionary conference in Cape Town; this eventually takes place (one hundred years later) in Edinburgh, Scotland. **[Africa: South Africa]**

1811 The British war with the Xhosa leads to the emergence of several prophet-leaders with differing responses to the injustices that the Xhosa faced; these include Makhanda Nxele, who encourages war against the whites, and Ntsikana, who advocates a retreat into a mystical indigenous form of African Christianity. **[Africa: South Africa]**

1811 The German LMS missionary Heinrich Schmelen begins his missionary work among the nomadic Nama tribes of South Africa and Namibia, trekking with them to |Ui≠gandes near the Atlantic coast, where he builds a mission station which he names Bethanie; his cottage there, erected in 1814, is long regarded as the oldest surviving building in Namibia (although the ruined fortifications at ǁKhauxa!nas predate European settlement).³ **[Africa: Namibia]**

1813 American Baptist missionary Adoniram Judson arrives in Burma, but initially has little success, not baptizing his first convert (Maung Naw) until six years later. **[Asia: Myanmar (Burma)]**

1813 Krishna Chandra Pol, William Carey's first baptized Hindu convert, becomes the first Protestant missionary among the headhunter hill tribes of Northeastern India (Assam and Meghalaya). **[Asia: India]**

1813 The condemnation of the East India Company's antimissionary attitudes leads to the British Government's passing of the Charter of 1813, establishing an Anglican church structure in India and permitting missionary work among Indians. **[Asia: India]**

1814 Methodist pioneer Thomas Coke and a party of four Methodist missionaries launch the first sustained organized Protestant mission

---

3. The symbols |, ≠, ǁ, and ! represent "click" sounds in the Khoikhoi language.

in Galle; however, Coke himself does not reach Sri Lanka, dying on the long voyage out. [**Asia: Sri Lanka**]

1814 Samuel Marsden preaches a Christmas Day sermon to Māori at Oihi Bay, Bay of Islands, marking the beginning of the CMS mission in New Zealand. [**Oceania: New Zealand**]

1815 Dutch missionary Joseph Carel Kam arrives in Amboina (Ambon) to begin work in the Moluccas (initially under the LMS, but later under the Dutch NZG), where he evangelizes pagans, revitalizes churches, and trains national leaders and missionaries to other Indonesian islands over the next twenty years. [**Asia: Indonesia**]

1815 The focus of the LMS mission in Tahiti shifts to the Leeward Islands (Raiatea, Huahine, and Borabora), which become the center of the Tahitian church and of future expansion in the Pacific. [**Oceania: French Polynesia**]

1815 The Unitarian Controversy emerges in the United States, resulting in a rational-minded church movement, organized as a split off from American Congregationalism; this Unitarianism minimizes the supernatural, instead emphasizing the benevolence of the One God and the moral goodness of humans. [**North America: United States of America**]

1816 The creation of the Zulu Empire under Shaka contributes to the Mfecane (Zulu: lit. "grinding," i.e. the mass migration of tribes fleeing Zulu expansion from 1820 on), and ultimately to the wider spread of Christianity across Southern Africa. [**Africa: South Africa**]

1816 The LMS missionary William Milne baptizes the young Hakka Chinese convert Liang Fa in Malacca; Robert Morrison later ordains him in 1824 as an evangelist, thus making him the first official Chinese Protestant missionary to his own people. [**Asia: China**]

1817 Ann Hasseltine Judson, wife of Adoniram Judson, the pioneer missionary to Burma, translates the first Scripture portion (from the Gospel of Matthew) and her husband's Burmese Catechism into Thai. [**Asia: Myanmar (Burma), Thailand**]

1817 John Williams arrives in Tahiti as part of a group of young and energetic LMS missionaries; after working under older missionaries in Moorea for some months, they move westward to the islands in the

Leeward group (Raiatea, Huahine, and Borabora) where the LMS is beginning to focus its efforts. [**Oceania: French Polynesia**]

1817 Scottish LMS missionary Robert Moffat arrives in South Africa to begin fifty-three years' missionary work; four years after his arrival, he sets up a mission station at Kuruman, which becomes a flourishing oasis (due to the local springs and to Moffat's models of irrigation) and a model for other mission stations, although the Christian community there remains small. [**Africa: South Africa**]

1818 The first in a series of mass movements toward Christianity begins in India among the Nadar lower-caste palm-wine carriers ("toddy-drawers") in Tamil Nadu, led by Maharasan Vedamanikam, a converted Dalit ("untouchable"); this results in rapid church growth among the LMS mission churches in Tamil Nadu. [**Asia: India**]

1819 A group of St. Joseph of Cluny sisters, the first group of women missionaries in Africa, settle on Gorée Island, Senegal; however, Mother Javouhey, their foundress, only stays four years, being invalided home to France in 1823, where King Louis Phillipe pays her the highest praise he could think of: "*Madame Javouhey! Mais c'est un grand homme*! [Madame Javouhey! But she's a great man!]" [**Africa: Senegal**]

1819 After much delay, due to their doubts about the genuineness of his conversion, the LMS missionaries eventually baptize Pōmare II, chief of much of Tahiti, in the royal chapel at Papeete. [**Oceania: French Polynesia**]

1819 Sir Stamford Raffles, ambitious colonialist and former Lieutenant-Governor of Java during its rule by the British from 1811 to 1815, lands on an undeveloped island at the end of the Malaysian peninsula and establishes a post there that lays the foundations of the modern state of Singapore. [**Asia: Singapore**]

1820 Hiram Bingham and a party of New England American missionaries begin work in Hawai'i; a second group of missionaries and Tahitian converts arrive later that year to assist them. [**Oceania: (Hawai'i)**]

1820 King William I of the Netherlands instructs the different Indonesian churches to unite into a single Protestant Reformed Church body, the Protestantsche Kerk in Nederlandsch-Indië (Protestant [State] Church of the Netherlands Indies), over which he would have indirect control through the Governor-General. [**Asia: Indonesia**]

A Timeline of Global Christianity

1820 LMS Missionaries arrive in Madagascar at the invitation of its king Radama I and establish a mission enterprise that flourishes in the decades that follow, in spite of persecution after Radama's death in 1828. [**Africa: Madagascar**]

1820 Scottish missionary Dr. John Philip becomes the LMS superintendent at the Cape Colony, remaining in this role until his death, but attracting enduring hostility from the settlers for his sustained opposition to their oppression of the natives. [**Africa: South Africa**]

1821 LMS missionary John Williams sends two Raiatean missionaries (Papeiha and Vahapata) to Aitutaki, in the Cook Islands; the use of Tahitian and other Pacific Island converts to make the initial approaches to new island groups and societies becomes a characteristic of missionary work in the Pacific. [**Oceania: Cook Islands**]

1821-1841 The rigidly Confucian Emperor Minh Mạng begins a brutal persecution, imprisoning, torturing, and executing missionaries, including Ignatius Delgado (the Vicar Apostolic of East Tonkin) and Vietnamese Christians, as well as demolishing churches. [**Asia: Viet Nam**]

1822 Samuel and Catherine Leigh arrive in New Zealand to begin Wesleyan missions and, together with fellow Wesleyan missionary William White, establish a mission station at Wesleydale, near Kaeo, in 1823. [**Oceania: New Zealand**]

1822 The American Colonization Society, established in 1816 by Presbyterian minister Robert Finlay and other influential figures in the white community to facilitate the transporting of freeborn blacks and emancipated slaves from America to the west coast of Africa, sets up a colony at Cape Mesurado, Liberia. [**Africa: Liberia**]

1823 John Williams leads an exploratory voyage from Raiatea to the southern Cook Islands in the missionary vessel *Endeavour*; the LMS later commemorates his missionary voyages by successively naming seven of its missionary ships after him. [**Oceania: Cook Islands**]

1823 The antislavery LMS missionary John Smith dies in prison, apparently of ill health, while awaiting execution after aiding a slave revolt in Demerara; his death reinforces the movement to abolish slavery. [**Latin America and the Caribbean: Guyana**]

1824 Brazil's creole clergy revolt against the traditional colonial models of ecclesiastical authority, although Catholicism remains the official religion of an independent Brazil. [**Latin America and the Caribbean: Brazil**]

1824 The American Presbyterian revivalist (and lawyer by training) Charles Grandison Finney introduces his "New Measures" Revivalism in upstate New York; his writings in the 1830s widely disseminate his views on the promotion of revivals by human agency. [**North America: United States of America**]

1824 The powerful Queen Regent Ka'ahumanu professes belief in Christianity and, together with six high chiefs, requests baptism from the American missionaries; her conversion prompts her subjects to follow suit. [**Oceania: (Hawai'i)**]

1824–1826 The first Anglo-Burmese War leads to the expansion of the British Empire into Burma and, indirectly, to the arrest of missionaries Adoniram Judson, Dr. Jonathan Price and a number of other Westerners and sepoy soldiers, and to their twenty-one months of great suffering in prison. [**Asia: Myanmar (Burma)**]

1826 After an unsuccessful attempt by Walter Lawry and others to introduce Methodism in Tonga in 1822–1823, the Wesleyan mission recommences under John Thomas. [**Oceania: Tonga**]

1826 Ko Thah A, one of Adoniram Judson's first converts, becomes the first pastor of the Burmese Baptist church in Rangoon (Yangon) and, as such, the first ordained Burmese minister. [**Asia: Myanmar (Burma)**]

1826–1830s Many newly independent liberal South and Central American governments suppress the Catholic religious orders (dominated by loyalist Spanish priests) throughout Latin America; this reinforces the exodus of many *peninsulares* (priests identified with Spanish interests) after independence. [**Latin America and the Caribbean: Argentina, Plurinational State of Bolivia, Bolivarian Republic of Venezuela, Chile, Colombia, Ecuador, Guatemala, Mexico, Nicaragua, Paraguay, Peru**]

1827 Judson converts the former Karen bandit Ko Thah Byu, who works with him and with George and Sarah Boardman to evangelize the

Karen tribe; Ko Thah Byu's success leads to his nickname of "the Karen Apostle." [**Asia: Myanmar (Burma)**]

1828 Four Swiss Basel missionaries come to Ghana in response to African invitations; three of them soon die due to the unhealthy environment in which they set up their mission, with the survivor, Andreas Riis, only being saved by the administrations of an African herbalist. [**Africa: Ghana**]

1829 After thirty years of crusading against the Hindu practice of sati (widow-burning) by William Carey, the British authorities prohibit it in their territories; the princely states follow suit in the following decades, with Queen Victoria issuing a general ban across the whole of India in 1861. [**Asia: India**]

1829 Khoikhoi settlers at the Kat River choose the LMS missionary James Read as their minister, thus forming the first independent black church (as distinct from mission) in South Africa. [**Africa: South Africa**]

1829 The British Parliament passes the Roman Catholic Relief Act 1829, which repeals the 1673 Test Act and thereby establishes Catholic emancipation in Britain. [**Europe: United Kingdom of Great Britain and Northern Ireland (England)**]

1830 A reaction to the increasing missionary impact of Christianity among Māori emerges in the Bay of Islands and the Hokianga in the form of Papahurihia, an adaptation cult that fuses Old Testament themes with Māori traditional religion. [**Oceania: New Zealand**]

1830 Joseph Smith founds the Church of Jesus Christ of Latter-day Saints (also unofficially known as the Mormons, due to their appeal to the *Book of Mormon* as a source of doctrine) in western New York State. [**North America: United States of America**]

1830 *The Protestant*, a magazine begun by several Protestant ministers, starts a Nativist (i.e. antiforeign) crusade against Catholic immigrants, seeing them as diluting America's Anglo-Saxon Protestant base and increasing its religious diversity; this antagonism culminates in brutal sectarian street confrontations, with hundreds of injuries, in Philadelphia in 1844. [**North America: United States of America**]

1830 The Wesleyan missionary John Thomas baptizes the high chief Tāufaʻāhau (the ruler of Haʻapai and later to become the king of all Tonga as George Tupou I). [**Oceania: Tonga**]

1830s John Williams (the first missionary to visit Samoa) and a handful of Cook Island and Tahitian missionaries preach in American Samoa and Tonga. [**Oceania: American Samoa, Tonga**]

1830s A Swiss Basel Mission missionary, Samuel Gobat, working under the auspices of the CMS, makes two brief sojourns in Ethiopia, where he seeks to reform Ethiopian religion to bring it more in line with Protestantism. [**Africa: Ethiopia**]

1833 The Bamokoteli chieftain Moshoeshoe invites members of the Paris Evangelical Missionary Society to Lesotho, although this is largely for economic and diplomatic, rather than religious, reasons; he finally seeks baptism on his deathbed in 1870. [**Africa: Lesotho**]

1833 The Oxford Movement begins in England with the publication of a series of ninety Anglo-Catholic theological publications (the *Tracts for the Times*) by leaders of the movement from 1833 to 1841; this series leads to the informal title of "Tractarians" for adherents of the movement. [**Europe: United Kingdom of Great Britain and Northern Ireland (England)**]

1833 Two American Protestant missionaries, Samuel Munson and Henry Lyman, arrive in Sumatra, but their mission is short lived, as a band of two hundred tribesmen kill them on their first trip into the Batak hill country the following year. [**Asia: Indonesia**]

1834 An American Presbyterian missionary, Peter Parker, opens a hospital in Guangzhou (thus pioneering the use of medicine as a missionary method) and works in China for twenty-three years, gaining a national reputation and eventually also being appointed to the diplomatic post of United States Commissioner to the Chinese Empire in 1844. [**Asia: China**]

1834 Justin Perkins, an American missionary in Northwest Persia, discovers the surviving remnants of the Nestorian Church (who he calls "the Protestants of Asia") around Urmia in the mountainous areas of Kurdistan. [**Asia: Islamic Republic of Iran (Persia)**]

1834 The "Tongan Revival," characterized by a classic Wesleyan focus on the "warmed heart" and a changed life, begins in Vava'u and sweeps south to the main Tongan island groups of Ha'apai and Tongatapu. [**Oceania: Tonga**]

1834 Three priests of the Congregation of the Sacred Hearts of Jesus and Mary (also known as the "Picpus Fathers," because of the location of the Order's first house on the Rue de Picpus in Paris) arrive in the Gambier Islands to begin Catholic missionary work in the Pacific. **[Oceania: French Polynesia]**

1834–1835 The Cape frontier war highlights differences in missionary attitudes toward the Xhosa, with Wesleyan missionary William Shrewsbury advocating driving back the Xhosa "invasion," and LMS superintendent John Philip opposing the war. **[Africa: South Africa]**

1835 After twenty-four years of labor, Adoniram Judson prints and publishes his translation of the Bible into Burmese. **[Asia: Myanmar (Burma)]**

1835 As a result of its links with Tonga and the Wesleyan mission there, and through the work of Wesleyans William Cross, David Cargill, and a number of Tongan missionaries, Fiji becomes the first Melanesian island group to receive Christianity. **[Oceania: Fiji]**

1835 Black Brazilians (i.e. repatriated Afro-Brazilian freed slaves) become influential in the growth of West African Christianity (a female example being Venossa de Jesus, who builds a church in Agoué, Benin). **[Africa: Benin]**

1835 Pioneer American missionary doctor Dan Beach Bradley arrives in Thailand, where he spends the rest of his life (thirty-eight years) in medical mission; this approach becomes a crucial factor in the expansion of Thai Christianity. **[Asia: Thailand]**

1835–1840 The first waves of the "Great Trek" of Boer pastoralists and Cape Dutch citizens leave the British controlled Cape Colony and move north into the interior of what is now South Africa, taking the Dutch Reformed faith with them. **[Africa: South Africa]**

1835–1861 The reigning chieftainess Ranavalona I, the widow of King Radama I, leads a hostile reaction against foreigners and Christians, apparently perceiving them as a subversive fifth column; nevertheless, the church survives during these years of persecution as a growing, self-propagating church, being led entirely by Malagasy Christians. **[Africa: Madagascar]**

1836 The first Protestant (Methodist) Tongan missionaries arrive on the island of 'Uvea (Wallis Island), but their aggressiveness causes the

'Uvean king Lavelua to suspect that they want to undermine local chiefly authority, and war breaks out between the Wallis Islanders and the missionary party. [**Oceania: Wallis and Futuna Islands**]

1836-1856 The Peruvian priest and liberal scholar Francisco de Paula González Vigil writes two multivolume defenses of the authority of governments and bishops against what he calls the "pretensions" of the Roman Curia; these works challenge the authoritarianism of the Catholic Church in both the political and religious spheres. [**Latin America and the Caribbean: Peru**]

1837 Several Catholic missionaries, including Pierre (Peter) Chanel, arrive on Wallis, where (in contrast to the Methodist missionaries killed there the previous year) they succeed in gaining the king's trust and establish a long-lasting Catholic work. [**Oceania: Wallis and Futuna Islands**]

1837-1839 The American missionary Titus Coan leads a passionate Charles Finney-style revival in Hawai'i, during which approximately one-third of the population are converted to Christianity. [**Oceania: (Hawai'i)**]

1838 Britain abolishes slavery in the British Caribbean, which (despite the Slavery Abolition Act of 1833) had continued as a six-year "apprenticeship" system forcing slaves to remain on their plantations. [**Latin America and the Caribbean: Trinidad and Tobago**]

1838 The Catholic Church consecrates Antony Dupuch as the first Catholic bishop of Algiers in modern times. [**Africa: Algeria**]

1838 French Marist Jean Baptiste Pompallier, the bishop of Moorea and Vicar-Apostolic of Western Oceania, arrives in New Zealand to begin Catholic missions and to organize the Catholic Church throughout the country. [**Oceania: New Zealand**]

1838 Methodist Eurafrican missionary Thomas Birch Freeman arrives in Ghana, where he sets up churches and schools; he also visits Togo and Benin, and later begins a mission in Nigeria. [**Africa: Benin, Ghana, Nigeria, Togo**]

1839 Cannibals on the island of Erromanga kill and eat the pioneering LMS missionary John Williams and his layman companion James Harris. [**Oceania: Vanuatu (New Hebrides)**]

1839 Korean authorities torture and behead the first two Western missionaries to Korea (Pierre-Philibert Maubant and Jacques-Honoré Chastan) and the first Apostolic Vicar, Bishop Laurent Imbert. [**Asia: Republic of Korea (South Korea)**]

1839 LMS missionary Aaron Buzacott sets up a theological college (Takamoa College) in the Cook Islands to train Rarotongan teachers for further expansion into Samoa and Melanesia. [**Oceania: Cook Islands**]

1839 Two Catholic missionaries, French Lazarist Justin de Jacobus and Italian Capuchin Guglielmo Massaja, begin work in Ethiopia. [**Africa: Ethiopia**]

1839–1842 The First Opium War begins between Britain and China, with China's defeat resulting in the opening up of the country for the opium trade and, paradoxically, for missionaries; up to this time, it had been legally impossible for missionaries to reside in China. [**Asia: China**]

1840 More than five hundred Māori chiefs sign the Treaty of Waitangi with representatives of the British Crown, leading to a declaration of British *kāwanatanga* (sovereignty) over New Zealand; missionaries are extensively involved in both the translation of the Treaty and persuading those Māori chiefs who had not been present at Waitangi to sign it. [**Oceania: New Zealand**]

1840 The LMS, under Thomas Heath and with the help of Samoan and Cook Islands missionaries, establishes Protestant missions on the Isle of Pines and in the Loyalty Islands. [**Oceania: New Caledonia**]

1840s German and Irish Catholic immigrants arrive in the United States, diluting its Anglo-Saxon Protestant base and increasing its religious diversity; this reinforces the Nativist campaign against such immigration and leads to outbreaks of violence. [**North America: United States of America**]

1841 A Futunan warrior, under instructions from King Niuliki, clubs the Marist missionary Pierre (Peter) Chanel to death. [**Oceania: Wallis and Futuna Islands**]

1841 The Glasgow Missionary Society founds the Lovedale Missionary Institute, an important educational institute in the development of African education, in Lovedale, Ciskei. [**Africa: South Africa**]

1841 The Niger Expedition sends three British vessels to the Niger River as part of a grandiose New Africa policy to make treaties with the native peoples, to introduce Christianity, and to promote increased trade. [**Africa: Nigeria**]

1841–1842 French Spiritan priest François-Marie-Paul Libermann founds the Congregation of the Sacred Heart of Mary as a mission to newly freed slaves in the French colonies, sending missionary Fathers Jacques-Desire Laval and Frédéric Le Vavasseur to Mauritius and Father Eugene Tisserant to Réunion; their success in these Indian Ocean islands secures a base for Catholic mission in Madagascar and throughout the whole of East Africa. [**Africa: Mauritius, Réunion; Europe: France**]

1842 The Ethiopian emperor expels all missionaries, including the German CMS missionary and explorer, Johann Ludwig Krapf; as a result, Krapf transfers his activities to Zanzibar and Kenya two years later. [**Africa: Ethiopia**]

1842 The first Protestant missionaries (from the ABCFM) arrive in Gabon; the first French Catholic missionaries (the Holy Ghost Fathers) follow them two years later. [**Africa: Gabon**]

1842 The islands of Wallis and Futuna become a French protectorate, resulting in a consolidation of French Catholic influence there. [**Oceania: Wallis and Futuna Islands**]

1843 The Anglican Church ordains Samuel Ajayi Crowther, previously well known for his role in the 1841 Niger Expedition, in England as its first African priest; he then returns to Africa to work in Yorubaland. [**Africa: Benin, Nigeria, Togo**]

1843 The arrival of a French gunboat alleviates (although it does not entirely halt) the persecution of Vietnamese Christians and French missionaries, leading eventually to the proclamation of a general amnesty for Christians in Viet Nam in 1847. [**Asia: Viet Nam**]

1843 The Danish philosopher Søren Kierkegaard publishes his first work *Enten-Eller* (*Either-Or*), an existential view of Christianity stressing the ethical imperatives of the maturing human conscience. [**Europe: Denmark**]

1843 The Great Disruption splits the Church of Scotland over the rights of its congregations to choose their ministers, rather than having the ministers presented to them by the local lairds. [**Europe: United Kingdom of Great Britain and Northern Ireland (Scotland)**]

1843–1844 Adventist groups in America and England, under the influence of William Miller, predict the Second Coming, but after the "Great Disappointment" when this did not happen, carry on with modified expectations, becoming the Seventh-day Adventists in 1863. [**North America: United States of America**]

1844 German mission pioneer Johann Ludwig Krapf arrives in Zanzibar and eventually sets up base in Mombasa, but has little missionary success (although he leaves a legacy in the study of the Swahili language). [**Africa: Kenya, United Republic of Tanzania**]

1844 German Pietist missionary Karl Gützlaff breaks with the NZG and sets up a short-lived Chinese Union of native evangelists and colporteurs, with the intention of fostering the growth of the Chinese Church under Chinese leadership. [**Asia: China**]

1844 LMS missionaries George Turner and Charles Hardie establish Malua Theological College, using the model of Takamoa College in the Cook Islands, to train missionary workers. [**Oceania: Samoa**]

1844 The Church of Jesus Christ of Latter-day Saints (Mormon) founder Joseph Smith sends his church's first foreign missionary, Addison Pratt, to French Polynesia. [**Oceania: French Polynesia**]

1844 The first Catholic missionaries (French Marists Jean-Baptiste Bréhéret and Joseph-François Roulleaux), arrive in Fiji and begin work at Lakeba in the southern Lau archipelago; Bréhéret becomes the first Prefect Apostolic of Fiji in 1863. [**Oceania: Fiji**]

1845 Editor John O'Sullivan coins the phrase "Manifest Destiny" in the July–August 1845 issue of the *Democratic Review*; this becomes an influential (although contested) idea that the United States would dominate its continent as a Christian republic. [**North America: United States of America**]

1845 The Baptists and Methodists in the southern states split off from their northern counterparts over the issue of slavery, leading to the formation of the Southern Baptist Convention in Atlanta, Georgia; this becomes the dominant church in the South and eventually the largest Protestant denomination in the United States in the second half of the twentieth century. [**North America: United States of America**]

1845 The Catholic Marist order arrives in Samoa and converts the prominent Samoan tulafale (orator-chief) Mata'afa Fagamanu, who ensures their protection from their Protestant rivals. [**Oceania: Samoa**]

1845 The Evangelical Oxford University scholar and Anglican priest John Henry Newman converts to the Roman Catholic Church, becoming one of its foremost leaders and theologians in the late nineteenth century. [**Europe: United Kingdom of Great Britain and Northern Ireland (England)**]

1845 The Marist order sends seven priests and six lay brothers to begin a mission in the Solomon Islands, but this soon founders due to native hostility and to their failure to understand the local cultures. [**Oceania: Solomon Islands**]

1845–1863 Tokelauan refugees fleeing a devastating hurricane reach Wallis; their conversion to Catholicism launches the Tokelauan Catholic mission, although there are also LMS Samoan Protestants working in Atafu at the same time. [**Oceania: Tokelau**]

1846 A succession of Christian missions begins in the New Hebrides, with the Presbyterians arriving in 1846, the Anglican Melanesian Mission in 1860, and the French Catholic Marists in 1887. [**Oceania: Vanuatu (New Hebrides)**]

1846 A vicious, but short-lived, persecution breaks out in Korea, with three missionaries and seventy-five Christians losing their lives, including the first Korean priest, Andrew Kim Tae-Kon. [**Asia: Republic of Korea (South Korea)**]

1846 Black and white Christians from Jamaica, led by Scottish Missionary Society missionary Hope M. Waddell, found the United Presbyterian mission in Calabar; this mission later becomes famous for Mary Slessor's long residence there. [**Africa: Nigeria**]

1846 The Vatican appoints the Maltese prelate Annetto Casolini as the first Apostolic Vicar of Central Africa; following his appointment, Casolini leads a mission to the Sudan, reaching the Nile valley and Khartoum in 1848. [**Africa: Sudan**]

1846 The Vatican subdivides Ethiopia into two Apostolic Vicariates, with the Lazarists receiving the responsibility for Abyssinia and the Capuchins, for Galla. [**Africa: Ethiopia**]

1847 A group of Spanish Benedictine monks under Rosendo Salvado and Joseph Serra set up a monastery (New Norcia) on the west coast of Australia in an attempt to evangelize the Aboriginals. [**Oceania: Australia**]

1847 Following the assassination in 1844 of Joseph Smith, the founder of the Church of Jesus Christ of Latter-day Saints (Mormons), and ongoing conflict with its neighbors, Brigham Young leads a migration of the Church from Nauvoo, Illinois to Salt Lake City, Utah. [**North America: United States of America**]

1847 Liberia achieves political independence from America as the first African country to gain independence from the colonial powers. [**Africa: Liberia**]

1847 Seven years after first arriving in Africa, David Livingstone reaches Kolobeng, Botswana, his third and final mission station; while here, he converts his only African convert, Sechele I, the Kgosi (hereditary leader) of the Bakwena tribe, to Christianity. [**Africa: Botswana**]

1847 The High Church Anglo-Catholic Robert Gray becomes the first bishop of Cape Town, but later clashes with the Low Church Evangelical bishop of Natal, John Colenso, over the issue of Biblical criticism. [**Africa: South Africa**]

1848 German philosophers and political theorists Karl Marx and Friedrich Engels jointly publish *The Communist Manifesto*, a comprehensive view of history as a series of class struggles leading to the revolutionary overthrow of the bourgeoisie (the ruling class) by the proletariat (the working classes), the abolition of capitalism, and the rise of socialism (and ultimately of communism). [**Europe: Germany**]

1849 A long-lasting schism develops in Sri Lankan Catholicism between Indian Goanese and European priests, lasting until 1940. [**Asia: Sri Lanka**]

1849 New Zealand Anglican missionaries set up the Melanesian Mission in the Solomon Islands. [**Oceania: Solomon Islands**]

1850 Russian Orthodox missionary work resumes along the Yenisei River around Turukhansk in central Siberia among the Tunguz, Yakuts, and Samoyed tribes. [**Asia: Russian Federation (Siberia)**]

1850–1864 The Taiping Rebellion, an adaptation of Protestant Christianity by Chinese scholar Hong Xiuquan and his followers, breaks out; this conflict over what is effectively a form of semi-Christian Messianism lasts for fourteen years and takes an estimated twenty million lives. [**Asia: China**]

1850s The ABCFM establishes strong missions on Kosrae and Pohnpei. [**Oceania: Federated States of Micronesia, Marshall Islands**]

1851 A fanatically anti-Christian antiforeign Chinese secret society, the Hong Brotherhood, kills about five hundred Chinese (most of whom are Catholic) in Singapore. [**Asia: Singapore**]

1851 The accession of King Mongkut (Rama IV, popularly known in the West as the King in *Anna and the King of Siam*) to the Siamese throne brings new openness toward the Christian mission in Thailand. [**Asia: Thailand**]

1852 Paulo, a Samoan LMS missionary, establishes a Congregationalist church on Niue after several unsuccessful attempts by other LMS landing parties. [**Oceania: Niue**]

1852 The establishment of the Holy Synod in Greece (modelled after that set up in the Russian Orthodox Church in 1721) brings about the independence of the Greek Orthodox Church from the Ecumenical Patriarch of Constantinople, a process known as "autocephaly." [**Europe: Greece**]

1852 The first Protestant missionaries (Hiram Bingham II, an American-Hawaiian, and J. W. Kanoa, a Hawaiian) arrive in Kiribati. [**Oceania: Kiribati**]

1853 A Baptist Missionary Convention of missionaries and Burmese Christian leaders meets in Rangoon (Yangon) to plan a fifty-year strategy, deciding on three key emphases: the development of self-supporting and self-propagating national leadership, the formation of a partnership between medical work and mission, and the extension of a network of nationally led and self-supporting Christian schools. [**Asia: Myanmar (Burma)**]

1853–1856 David Livingstone, the first European to cross the African continent, begins his explorations of the African interior; however, this transcontinental journey had been attempted fifty years previously by two African *pombeiros* (agents of Portuguese merchants).

[Africa: Angola, Democratic Republic of the Congo, Malawi, Mozambique, United Republic of Tanzania, Zambia, Zimbabwe]

1854 Pope Pius IX issues the papal bull *Ineffabilis Deus*, establishing the dogma of the immaculate conception of the Virgin Mary as an article of Catholic faith; this is one of only two ex cathedra papal pronouncements (which the Catholic Church considers to be infallible, since they articulate the teaching authority of the Church), the other being Pope Pius XII's definition in 1950 of the dogma of the assumption of the Virgin Mary. [**Europe: Italy**]

1854 The Japanese sign a treaty with the United States, opening up the country to Westerners; the establishment of three treaty ports for foreigners five years later enables missionaries to take advantage of these new opportunities. [**Asia: Japan**]

1854 The Methodist missionary James Calvert converts Chief Seru Epenisa Cakobau to Christianity; the Chief's conversion, and his consequent renunciation of polygamy and cannibalism, leads to the establishment of a strong Methodist church in Fiji. [**Oceania: Fiji**]

1855 The CMS Honorary Secretary Henry Venn formulates his Three-Self principle (in which CMS-founded churches should become self-supporting, self-governing, and self-propagating), the aim being that missions should ideally be temporary, and that the national churches should become indigenous, and not encumbered with paternalistic European "cultural baggage." [**Europe: United Kingdom of Great Britain and Northern Ireland (England)**]

1855 The Dajazmach (Commander of the Gate) Kasa seizes the Imperial throne, taking the messianic name Tewodros (Theodore, or "Gift of God"), and (in his words) seeking to "reform Abyssinia, restore the Christian faith and become master of the world." [**Africa: Ethiopia**]

1856 A schism emerges in the Baptist mission in Burma over the increasingly inflexible control of the Missionary Union board in America; this control vitiates the independent decision-making ability of missionaries on the field, particularly among the Karen tribes. [**Asia: Myanmar (Burma)**]

1856 After walking west to east across Africa from Luanda to Quelimane, David Livingstone returns to England, fueling immense excitement about opportunities for "commerce and Christianity" in Africa. [**Africa: Angola, Mozambique, Zambia, Zimbabwe**]

1856 The Congregation for the Propagation of the Faith assigns the responsibility for the Catholic mission in Burma to the Paris Foreign Mission Society. [**Asia: Myanmar (Burma)**]

1857 A Sgaw Karen convert, Saw Quala, takes over the leadership of the Baptist mission among the Karen tribes on missionary Francis Mason's return home due to ill health, and leads the mission to sustained growth. [**Asia: Myanmar (Burma)**]

1857 After several decades of persecution in Madagascar (during which time Christians are forced to go into hiding, to flee to the Malagasy countryside, or to take refuge on the neighboring islands of Mauritius, Réunion, and Nosy-Bé), oppression of the Christians begins to diminish, finally ending in 1861. [**Africa: Madagascar, Mauritius, Réunion**]

1857 As part of the major reforms introduced under its minister of justice, Benito Pablo Juárez Garcia, the new liberal government of Mexico temporarily deposes Catholicism as the state religion. [**Latin America and the Caribbean: Mexico**]

1857 Despite sharing a similar Reformed faith, white Boer Christians now require the Coloreds (i.e. the Griquas) to worship in separate chapels from the Europeans. [**Africa: South Africa**]

1857 Samuel Ajayi Crowther becomes the leader of the Niger Mission, but this later declines when a committee of Europeans undercuts his authority and takes over the Mission's "temporalities" in 1879; it had become effectively defunct by the time of Crowther's death in 1891. [**Africa: Nigeria**]

1857 The ABCFM sends two missionary couples (Edward and Sarah Doane, and George and Nancy Pierson) to Ebon, in the south of the Marshall Islands. [**Oceania: Marshall Islands**]

1857 The publication of David Livingstone's best-selling book *Missionary Travels and Researches in South Africa* reinforces his public reputation as a heroic explorer, who had made contributions to geography, medicine, and science, as well as to missionary work and the abolition of the slave trade. [**Africa: South Africa**]

A Timeline of Global Christianity

1857–1858 A yearlong rebellion begins in Britain's Indian Army (the "Indian Mutiny"); its defeat the following year results in the British government taking complete control of British interests in India, and in the start of the British Raj, which lasts until Indian independence in 1947. [**Asia: India**]

1858 Livingstone's influence helps to create the Universities' Mission to Central Africa, an Anglican enterprise having as its initial objective Lake Nyasa and the Shiré Valley; this particular mission field comes to be known as "Livingstonia." [**Africa: Malawi**]

1858 Roman Catholic missionaries (Fathers Ausoleil and Triaire, and several companions) attempt to enter Laos from Cambodia with the intention of setting up a mission at Luang Prabang in Central Laos; however, almost all of the missionaries die from forest fever, leading to the abandoning of the mission. [**Asia: Lao People's Democratic Republic**]

1859 The English naturalist Charles Darwin publishes his seminal book *On the Origin of Species*, a work of scientific literature considered to be the foundation of evolutionary biology. [**Europe: United Kingdom of Great Britain and Northern Ireland (England)**]

1860 As a result of French intervention following the massacre of eleven thousand Christians in Lebanon and Damascus, Syria and Lebanon become an autonomous province with a Christian governor, while remaining part of the Ottoman Empire. [**Asia: Lebanon, Syrian Arab Republic**]

ca.1860 A German LMS missionary baptizes Kgama, who later becomes Kgosi Kgama III of the Ngwato, founding a Christian state with a well-organized, well-funded independent government dominated by Christians. [**Africa: Botswana**]

ca.1860 The circulation of Bibles in Eritrea by the British and Foreign Bible Society leads to the emergence of an Eritrean religious movement similar to a Protestant Reformation. [**Africa: Eritrea**]

1860–1875 Ecuador's president Gabriel Garcia Moreno presides over one of most staunchly Catholic administrations in Latin American history; his reformist dictatorship is based upon the premise that Ecuador's political and economic difficulties would be resolved by the application of moral principles by a powerful leader. [**Latin America and the Caribbean: Ecuador**]

1861 Elekana, a deacon of the LMS church in Manuhiki (Cook Islands) drifts on to Tuvalu while at sea during a storm; after preaching to the Tuvaluans, he returns four years later as leader of a Cook Island/Samoan missionary team. [**Oceania: Tuvalu**]

1861 The establishment of a CMS Native Pastorate marks the first step toward a self-governing national Church and the "euthanasia" of mission in Sierra Leone. [**Africa: Sierra Leone**]

1861 The recently enthroned king Radama II proclaims religious freedom, releases imprisoned Christians, and enables LMS missions to return to Madagascar; Catholics, Anglicans, Norwegian Lutherans, and Quakers also arrive to begin missionary work. [**Africa: Madagascar**]

1861–1865 The American Civil War breaks out between the eleven slave-owning southern Confederate states and the twenty loyalist Union states in the North; despite their differing perspectives on slavery, each side claims a strong religious base for its ideology. [**North America: United States of America**]

1862 The German Pietist Ludwig Nommensen arrives in Sumatra and works among the Bataks for fifty-six years, thereby helping to make the Batak Christian Protestant Church one of the largest and fastest-growing indigenous churches in Asia. [**Asia: Indonesia**]

1863 Bishop Robert Gray of Cape Town deposes his colleague, Bishop John Colenso of Natal, for his liberal views on Biblical criticism, but the Privy Council overturns this decision on an appeal. [**Africa: South Africa**]

1863 President Abraham Lincoln issues the Emancipation Proclamation abolishing slavery in the southern Confederate-controlled states; abolition extends nationwide with the Thirteenth Amendment to the Constitution, ratified in 1865. [**North America: United States of America**]

1864 The Anglican Universities' Mission to Central Africa relocates to Zanzibar after a disastrous failure to establish a mission in Malawi in 1861, later founding new missions on the mainland from this base. [**Africa: Malawi, United Republic of Tanzania**]

1864 Two French priests (Holy Ghost Fathers Edward Blanchet and Joseph Koeberle), together with an Irish lay brother, arrive in Freetown, Sierra Leone to begin Catholic missions. [**Africa: Sierra Leone**]

1864 Yoruba clergyman and linguist Samuel Ajayi Crowther, already well-known as the leader of the Niger Mission, becomes bishop of the Niger, the mother diocese of the Church of Nigeria and, as such, the first black Anglican bishop in West Africa. [**Africa: Nigeria**]

1865 Despite opposition to the Gospel from the Tokugawa Shōgunate, American Protestant missionaries in Yokohama baptize Yano Ryūsan (Yano Mototaka), their first Japanese convert. [**Asia: Japan**]

1865 Maverick English evangelist and former Methodist minister William Booth launches the Christian Mission (later renamed the Salvation Army) in the East End of London, offering practical help to the poor and destitute, in addition to preaching the Gospel. [**Europe: United Kingdom of Great Britain and Northern Ireland (England)**]

1865 The British Protestant missionary Hudson Taylor initiates the China Inland Mission (CIM) as an interdenominational faith mission, with its first missionaries arriving in China the following year; this had become the largest Protestant mission in China by 1900, with more than one thousand CIM missionaries on the field. [**Asia: China**]

1865 The French Catholic missionary Bernard Petitjean finds that scattered remnants of the communities founded by the Jesuits in Nagasaki in seventeenth-century Japan had survived, retaining some thirty thousand Kakure Kirishitan (hidden Christians), but also that their Christianity had been assimilated with folk superstitions and had been changed almost out of all recognition. [**Asia: Japan**]

1865 Welsh Congregationalist missionary Robert Jermain Thomas spends two and a half months in Korea, but dies on his attempted return there in 1866 when the American schooner on which he is travelling strands in forbidden waters near Pyongyang and is set on fire by Korean fire arrows, killing all on board. [**Asia: Democratic People's Republic of Korea (North Korea)**]

1866–1867 Korean authorities order the complete eradication of Catholic Christians in the country, killing eight thousand Christians, with many more dying from starvation and deprivation over the next three years. [**Asia: Democratic People's Republic of Korea (North Korea), Republic of Korea (South Korea)**]

1867 The Archbishop of Canterbury, Charles Thomas Longley, presides over the first decennial Conference of Anglican bishops at Lambeth Palace; seventy-six of the 144 bishops in the Anglican Communion are present. [**Europe: United Kingdom of Great Britain and Northern Ireland (England)**]

1867 The Mexican government under the anti-Catholic reformer Benito Pablo Juárez Garcia overthrows the Second Mexican Empire, executes Maximilian I (briefly the Emperor of Mexico), and re-implements the anticlerical laws previously passed in the 1850s. [**Latin America and the Caribbean: Mexico**]

1868 All of the LMS-associated Protestant congregations in Madagascar combine to form the Madagascar Congregational Union (the Isan-enim-bolana; lit. "every six months," a reference to their half-yearly meetings) as a step toward an autonomous Malagasy church. [**Africa: Madagascar**]

1868 French Archbishop Charles Lavigerie of Algiers (later to become Cardinal Archbishop of Carthage and the primate of Africa) founds the Society of Missionaries of Africa (the White Fathers) in Algeria. [**Africa: Algeria**]

1868 Pope Pius IX summons the First Vatican Council, which meets from December 1869 to October 1870; among the Council's decrees is the dogma of papal infallibility (i.e. that when the pope speaks ex cathedra in definition of the Church's doctrine, faith, or morals, he articulates the mind of the Church and is therefore preserved from the possibility of error). [**Europe: Italy**]

1868 Ranavalona II (widow of King Radama II, murdered in 1863) becomes the Queen of Madagascar and approves Protestant missionary work in her country. [**Africa: Madagascar**]

1870 Somdet Chao Phraya Si Suriyawong, the reform-minded regent of the young King Chulalongkorn, proclaims a royal decree of religious toleration in Thailand. [**Asia: Thailand**]

1871 Welsh explorer and journalist Sir Henry Morton Stanley encounters Livingstone (who had been out of contact with the outside world for six years) at Ujiji on the shores of Lake Tanganyika, with the famous phrase "Doctor Livingstone, I presume?" [**Africa: United Republic of Tanzania**]

1871 Working from a recently established base on Darnley Island in the Torres Straits, LMS missionaries begin to engage in successful coastal and outer-island evangelism, especially on the south coast of Papua New Guinea. [**Oceania: Papua New Guinea**]

1872 Māori prophet Te Kooti Arikirangi Te Turuki experiences visions during his exile on the Chatham Islands, east of New Zealand, from 1865 to 1868; he later becomes a religious leader and sets up Te Hahi Ringatu (The Church of the Upraised Hand), basing this on Māori understandings of the Bible. [**Oceania: New Zealand**]

1872 An uprising at Fort San Felipe in Cavite results in the execution of Filipino nationalist priests José Burgos, Mariano Goméz, and Jacinto Zamora, and eventually leads to the Philippine Revolution of 1896. [**Asia: Philippines**]

1872 The Questão Religiosa ("Religious Question") erupts when a Brazilian bishop attempts to expel Freemasons from Catholic Lay Fraternities; this challenges both the Prime Minister, Baron Rio Branco (who is himself a Masonic Grand Master), and the Brazilian Emperor Pedro II, who had previously forbidden the promulgation within Brazil of a papal decree banning Catholic participation in Masonic associations. [**Latin America and the Caribbean: Brazil**]

1873 A public debate, attended by four to six thousand people, takes place in Panadura between the Christian Pali scholar David Wickrametilleke de Silva and the militantly anti-Christian Buddhist monk Mohottivatte Gunananda Thera; however, de Silva's arguments prove too intellectual for the audience and Gunananda's triumph in the debate leads to the resurgence of Sinhalese Buddhism in Sri Lanka. [**Asia: Sri Lanka**]

1873 David Livingstone dies, from malaria and hemorrhoids, at Chitambo, Zambia, where his two coworkers, Susi and Chuma, remove his heart and viscera, burying these under a tree close to the location of his death, preserving the remainder of his body, and then carrying it on foot to the coast (a journey of nine months), at last carefully laying it on the porch of the church in Bagamoyo with the simple words

"*Mwili wa Daudi* [David's body]"; it is then returned to Britain for eventual burial in Westminster Abbey. [**Africa: Zambia**]

1873 The American evangelist Dwight L. Moody, accompanied by his musician/hymnwriter partner, Ira D. Sankey, begins an enormously successful two-year preaching tour of Britain, with crowds of thousands attending his meetings. [**Europe: United Kingdom of Great Britain and Northern Ireland (England, Northern Ireland, Scotland)**]

1873 As a result of Western diplomatic pressure, the Meiji Imperial Court removes the last remaining anti-Christian edicts, although Christianity remains technically illegal in Japan until the restoration of freedom of worship in 1889. [**Asia: Japan**]

1874 Sir Henry Morton Stanley returns to Uganda, teaching the principles of the Christian faith to King Mutesa I Walugembe Mukaabya of Buganda, thereby creating opportunities for later missionaries. [**Africa: Uganda**]

1875 After serving as a missionary in Samoa for fourteen years, English Methodist minister George Brown sets up the first permanent mission station in the Bismarck Archipelago northeast of New Guinea, commencing work among the local Tolai people, who today remember him as a prophet. [**Oceania: Papua New Guinea**]

1875 The elderly Lao Christian Nan Inta, a well-respected former Buddhist abbot, becomes the first ordained northern Thai elder in Chiangmai. [**Asia: Thailand**]

1876 Lee [Yi] Ung-Ch'an becomes the first baptized Korean Protestant at the Scottish mission in Mukden, China, across the border from Korea; three other Koreans (Paik Hong-Chun, Lee [Yi] Song-Ha, and Kim Chin-Ki) also receive baptism about the same time. [**Asia: Democratic People's Republic of Korea (North Korea)**]

1876 Under Jean-Louis Vey, the Apostolic Vicar of Siam, the first successful Catholic mission enters Laos; Fathers Prodhomme and Perraux baptize forty Laotians in their first year in the country. [**Asia: Lao People's Democratic Republic**]

1877 The CMS establishes Protestant missions in Buganda (a subnational kingdom in Uganda); the success of these marks the turn of the tide for East African missionary work. [**Africa: Uganda**]

A Timeline of Global Christianity

1878 The Council of Boru-Meda, under the new Emperor Yohannes IV, attempts to resolve the long-standing Christological divisions in the Ethiopian church, bring about Muslim conversions, and rebuild Ethiopia. [**Africa: Ethiopia**]

1878 The English Baptists set up a chain of mission stations extending along fifteen hundred kilometers of the Congo River from Lake Malebo to Kisangani. [**Africa: Congo, Democratic Republic of the Congo**]

1879 The Serbian Orthodox Church regains its independence from Greek Phanariot control (i.e. the control of the Church by prominent Greek families in Phanar, the location of the Ecumenical Patriarchate), and again becomes autocephalous (completely independent in administrative matters). [**Europe: Bosnia and Herzegovina, Croatia, Montenegro, North Macedonia, Serbia**]

1879 on Intense missionary rivalry emerges between the Protestant CMS missionaries and the Catholic White Fathers in the Buganda royal court, and also between the embryonic Bugandan congregations; particular issues include the misuse of the Bible by inexperienced catechumens and the place of the title "Mary, Mother of God" in prayer and worship. [**Africa: Uganda**]

1880s Protestant church membership in Japan grows exponentially throughout the decade, with the Presbyterian, Reformed, and Congregationalist churches becoming the largest Japanese denominations. [**Asia: Japan**]

1880s The Church of Ethiopia makes several short-lived attempts to come into union with the Russian Orthodox Church, partly from religious motives and partly to offset the encroachment of French, British, and Italian imperialism. [**Africa: Ethiopia**]

1881 Charles Taze Russell founds the Zion's Watch Tower Tract Society (later renamed the Jehovah's Witnesses) for the purpose of distributing religious tracts; in the twentieth century, this grows to become a worldwide body, known for its aggressive evangelism. [**North America: United States of America**]

1881 The Māori prophet and teacher Erueti Te Whiti-o-Rongomai III develops a policy of non-violent passive resistance to widespread Pākeha (European) confiscation of Māori land at Parihaka and elsewhere, but

Pākeha authorities arrest him and his followers and, after an inconclusive trial for sedition and disturbance of the peace, detain them for two years. [**Oceania: New Zealand**]

1882 Korea (known as the "Hermit Kingdom" because of its isolation) begins to open to foreigners and to grant religious freedom; the first Protestant missionaries arrive in the country two years later. [**Asia: Democratic People's Republic of Korea (North Korea), Republic of Korea (South Korea)**]

1882 German Catholic missionaries begin work on New Britain Island (the largest in the Bismarck Archipelago, east of Papua New Guinea); after the annexation of the Archipelago by Germany in 1884, German Protestant missions follow two years later. [**Oceania: Papua New Guinea**]

1883 Evangelist Nehemiah Tile leaves the Wesleyan mission in the eastern Cape and sets up the Thembu National Church, the first independent African church and a forerunner of the African-Initiated Churches (AICs). [**Africa: South Africa**]

1883 Suh Sang-Yun assists in the translation of the Gospel of Luke in Mukden, China and later takes copies back to his home village, gathering a group of believers into the first Korean house church. [**Asia: China, Democratic People's Republic of Korea (North Korea)**]

1884 French occupation of Tunisia creates a favorable environment for the establishment of a Catholic hierarchy, leading to the revival of the ancient Archbishopric of Carthage. [**Africa: Tunisia**]

1885 A Catholic mass movement begins among the aboriginal tribes of Chota Nagpur under the Belgian Jesuit Constant Lievans, with more than sixty-five thousand conversions in four years. [**Asia: India**]

1885 Belgium's King Leopold II appropriates the Congo Free State as his personal possession, initiating a regime of egregious barbarity (beatings, mutilations, and the amputation of limbs being common punishments); he reinforces his colonial aspirations by permitting only Belgian Catholic missionaries to enter the country. [**Africa: Democratic Republic of the Congo**]

1885 The central and northern areas of Myanmar (formerly known as the kingdom of Ava, and broadly comprising the Mandalay, Sagaing, and Magway regions) lose their independence to Britain as result of the Third Anglo-Burmese War; the British then administer them as "Upper Burma," the easternmost province of India, until 1937. [**Asia: Myanmar (Burma)**]

1885 The Wallachian, Moldavian, and Transylvanian dioceses of the Constantinople patriarchate unite to become the Romanian Orthodox Church; this follows on from the political union of Moldavia and Wallachia to form the modern state of Romania twenty-six years earlier. [**Europe: Republic of Moldova, Romania, Ukraine**]

1886 Following the amalgamation of the Livingstone Inland Mission's and the Baptist Missionary Society's Congo missions two years earlier, a significant revival breaks out under Henry Richards at Banza Manteke, an awakening known as the "Pentecost on the Congo." [**Africa: Democratic Republic of the Congo**]

1886 The Ganda king Mwanga begins a violent local persecution of Christians in Buganda, resulting in a number of Catholic and Anglican martyrdoms; most of the victims are pages at the king's court, who had refused to submit to his desires for sodomy, and who suffered either maiming or burning to death. [**Africa: Uganda**]

1888 Hawaiian Protestant missionary influence declines in Kiribati as French-led Catholicism increases, largely at the instigation of native I-Kiribati from the island of Nonouti, who had converted to Catholicism while working as laborers in the European plantations on Tahiti. [**Oceania: Kiribati**]

1889 The fall of the Brazilian Empire and the deposition of Emperor Pedro II bring about a republican regime and, two years later, the enactment of a Constitution that separates church and state. [**Latin America and the Caribbean: Brazil**]

1890 Capt. Fredrick Lugard occupies Buganda for the Imperial British East Africa Company in order to preempt German influence in the area and to quell local disturbances between animists, Muslims, Protestants, Catholics, and the nominal Kabaka (king of Buganda) Mwanga II; Lugard's influence leads to Uganda becoming a British Protectorate in 1893. [**Africa: Uganda**]

1890 The first Seventh-day Adventist missionary in the Pacific, John I. Tay, visits Pitcairn and Fiji; as a result, virtually the entire population of Pitcairn becomes Seventh-day Adventist, and by the 1990s, the

Seventh-day Adventists had also become the largest nonmainstream religious group in the wider Pacific. [**Oceania: Fiji, Pitcairn**]

1890 Visiting China missionary John L. Nevius advises the Presbyterian mission to train the Korean church to be self-supporting, self-governing, and self-propagating from its very beginnings; this widely adopted "Three-Self" format (known as the "Nevius Plan" in Korea) is the primary factor in Presbyterian expansion there. [**Asia: Democratic People's Republic of Korea (North Korea), Republic of Korea (South Korea)**]

1891 Pope Leo XIII issues his encyclical *Rerum Novarum* on the social relationships, rights, and duties of Capital and Labor; this declaration lays a foundation for twentieth-century Catholic social teaching. [**Europe: Italy**]

1891 The enactment of Brazil's first Republican Constitution removes the status of official religion and disestablishes the Catholic Church; although the country has been secular ever since, the Catholic Church remained influential until the 1970s and a strong Catholic, Evangelical, and Pentecostal constituency continues among the Brazilian population. [**Latin America and the Caribbean: Brazil**]

1892 After receiving a series of visions that lead him to seek out an Arabic Bible, Muslim Shaikh Zakaryas of Begemdir begins to preach the necessity of reforming and renewing Islam, using the Bible to point out the shortcomings in the Qur'an; although he is strongly opposed by the local Muslim population, his message becomes more and more focused on conversion to Christianity, and eventually he and three thousand of his followers receive baptism in 1910. [**Africa: Ethiopia**]

1892 Methodist minister Mangena Maake Mokone founds an independent intertribal "Ethiopian Church," in South Africa, marking the beginning of African-led urban churches, in contrast to the earlier rural-based independent churches; these Ethiopian churches later amalgamate with the African Methodist Episcopal Church in the United States, thus internationalizing the movement. [**Africa: South Africa**]

1893 Charismatic Irish layman George Pilkington (a classical scholar and translator as well as an adherent of the Keswick movement) inspires a major revival in Buganda and Nyasaland (Malawi); an immediate fruit of this revival is the spread of Ganda evangelists into other tribal areas of Uganda and among the Pygmies of the Democratic Republic of the Congo. [**Africa: Democratic Republic of the Congo, Malawi, Uganda**]

1893 The first full Bible in Thai, based on American Baptist missionary John Taylor Jones's pioneering work, finally comes out fifty years after the publication of his Thai New Testament in 1843–1844. [**Asia: Thailand**]

1893 The World's Parliament of Religions meets in Chicago, marking the first formal gathering of representatives of Eastern and Western traditions and launching worldwide interreligious dialogue. [**North America: United States of America**]

1894–1895 The Japanese invasion of Korea leads to its independence from China and increasing Japanese colonial dominance in that country, lasting until 1945; this has the positive effect of creating opportunities for Western missions (providing a "noncolonial" alternative to Asian imperialism) and the rapid expansion of Christianity, particularly in the north, from 1897 on. [**Asia: Democratic People's Republic of Korea (North Korea), Republic of Korea (South Korea)**]

1894–1896 Genocidal pogroms begin in Constantinople under fanatical Sultan Abdul Hamid II, leading to the deaths of between one hundred thousand and three hundred thousand Armenians throughout Turkey; these massacres continue on a greater scale in 1915–1918. [**Asia: Armenia, Turkey**]

1895 Student leaders from ten European and North American countries meet at Vadstena Castle, Sweden, to form the World Student Christian Federation (WSCF), a federation of autonomous national Student Christian Movements. [**Europe: Sweden**]

1895 The number of Roman Catholics increases in Egypt, partly through immigration and partly by conversion of the Copts; this results in the formation of a Coptic Uniate church and the appointment of a Patriarch of Alexandria. [**Africa: Egypt**]

1896 Brazilian federal troops suppress the "Born Jesus" millennialist movement, led by miracle-worker Antônio Conselheiro, in a bloodbath at his community of Canudos; more than fifteen thousand people lose their lives in the massacre. [**Latin America and the Caribbean: Brazil**]

1896 Ethiopia's King Menelik II defeats an Italian army at the battle of Adowa, recognized throughout the entire African continent as a major victory against colonialism. [**Africa: Ethiopia**]

1898 The defeat of the Mahdī Muḥammad Ahmad bin Abd Allah in the Mahdist War leads to Sudan effectively becoming a British colony and to an influx of Christian missions; these have greater success in South Sudan than in the North. [**Africa: South Sudan, Sudan**]

1899 Following the American annexation of the Philippines, Protestant missionaries begin to arrive from the United States of America; however, only 3 percent to 4 percent of the Christian population had become Protestant between World War I and World War II. [**Asia: Philippines**]

1899 The Colegio Pio Latino-Americano Pontificio (Pontifical Latin American College) hosts a Plenary Council for Latin America at the Vatican, calling for reforms in the Latin American Catholic Church; this is the first major council of Latin American bishops presided over by their own archbishops. [**Latin America and the Caribbean**]

1899–1901 The antiforeign Yihequan (Boxer) Rebellion breaks out; this is not especially directed against Christians, churches, and missionaries, although 231 foreigners and tens of thousands of Chinese Christians are killed. [**Asia: China**]

1899–1914 This period of German colonization in Micronesia stimulates missionary activity, with Pohnpei receiving an influx of German missionary workers from the Evangelical Liebenzell Mission. [**Oceania: Federated States of Micronesia**]

1900 After working in Buganda for thirteen years, Alsatian missionary Bishop Jean-Joseph Hirth leads a group of White Fathers, together with twelve Ganda auxiliaries, into Rwanda to found a Catholic mission; however, their work there contains a strongly militaristic element due to their experience of more than a decade of violence in Buganda. [**Africa: Rwanda**]

1900 By the beginning of the twentieth century, only two countries in Asia (i.e. Lebanon and the Philippines) have a Christian religious majority in the population. [**Asia: Lebanon, Philippines**]

1900 New Guinea becomes a German protectorate; since Samoa is then also a German dominion, this increases opportunities for Samoan missionaries to work in the country. [**Oceania: Papua New Guinea, Samoa**]

1901 Pentecostalism emerges at Charles Fox Parham's Bible School in Topeka, Kansas, becoming a global movement through revival meetings at "Azusa Street" in Los Angeles five years later. [**North America: United States of America**]

1901 The White Fathers under Father Guillaume Templier arrive in Burkina Faso, establishing their base in the center of the capital Ouagadougou; however, despite building Catholic missions there and at Koupéla, and performing their first baptisms, they have only moderate success in the country. [**Africa: Burkina Faso**]

1902 Filipino priest Gregorio Aglipay advocates a nationalist secession from the Spanish-controlled church; when the church excommunicates him, he becomes the first bishop of the popular Iglesia Filipina Independiente (Philippine Independent Church, sometimes called the Aglipayan Church). [**Asia: Philippines**]

1902 French Protestant missionaries from the Société des missions évangéliques de Paris (Paris Evangelical Missionary Society) begin replacing the LMS Protestant missions in New Caledonia. [**Oceania: New Caledonia**]

1902 Pastor-ethnologist Maurice Leenhardt of the Paris Evangelical Missionary Society arrives in New Caledonia, where he develops a huge respect for the work of the earlier Kanak missionaries, and seeks to become the servant of the native-led churches, and to alleviate the "slow genocide" of the Kanak people. [**Oceania: New Caledonia**]

1903 Petrus Louis Le Roux, a former Dutch Reformed missionary to the Zulus, founds the Zionist Apostolic Church, integrating African cultural features and Pentecostal spirituality; this is one of the first African-Initiated Churches and expands to become a large network. [**Africa: South Africa**]

1903–1907 Revival begins at a missionary conference held in the Wonsan Methodist Church in 1903 and spreads to Pyongyang in 1905–1906; it culminates in the "Great Revival" (also called the "Manchurian Revival") which extends from Pyongyang throughout Korea and into China in 1907. [**Asia: China, Democratic People's Republic of Korea (North Korea)**]

1904 The Welsh Revival breaks out at the Moriah Calvinistic Methodist Church in Loughnor under the leadership of young trainee minister Evan Roberts and expands across Wales, gaining more than one hundred thousand converts over the next twelve months. [**Europe: United Kingdom of Great Britain and Northern Ireland (Wales)**]

1905 After twenty-four years of unproductive work by Plymouth Brethren missionaries, the outbreak of a religious awakening, remembered as Mwaka wa Lusa (The Year of Love), leads to the creation of important mission networks in Shaba and beyond. [**Africa: Angola, Democratic Republic of the Congo, Zambia**]

1905 During a period of Japanese nationalism under the Meiji regime (1890–1912), the Nihon Kumiai Kirisuto Kyokai (Japanese Congregational Church) becomes independent of Western missionary control, with other Japanese Protestant churches following its example. [**Asia: Japan**]

1905 The French Chamber des Députés passes Loi du 9 Décembre 1905 concernant la Séparation des Églises et de l'État (Law of 9 December, 1905, on the Separation of the Churches and the State), establishing state secularism; as a result, the French state takes over Church property. [**Europe: France**]

1908 The fiery radical Anglo-Catholic priest and educator Frank Weston becomes Bishop of Zanzibar; he has a particular concern for the traditional teaching and practice of the Church of England, and especially for the principle of episcopacy, which he sees as a defining characteristic of this Church as the English section of the universal Catholic Church. [**Africa: United Republic of Tanzania**]

1908 The Vatican redefines American Catholicism as being no longer under the Congregation for the Propagation of the Faith and hence no longer a "mission," but now a mature church in its own right. [**North America: United States of America**]

1909 Pentecostalism emerges in the Valparaiso congregation of Methodist Episcopal missionaries Willis and Minnie Hoover through the influence of Indian Pentecostal pioneer Pandita Ramabai's book *The Baptism of the Holy Ghost and Fire*; the Hoovers are also influential in fostering the beginnings of Pentecostalism in Argentina later that year. [**Latin America and the Caribbean: Argentina, Chile**]

A Timeline of Global Christianity

1910 During a three-year period of increasing tensions between Copts and Muslims (1908–1911), a Muslim member of the nationalist Waṭanī Party assassinates Egypt's only Coptic Christian Prime Minister, Pasha Boutros-Ghālī; his grandson Boutros Boutros-Ghālī would become the sixth Secretary-General of the United Nations eighty-two years later. [**Africa: Egypt**]

1910 Self-styled prophet Isaiah Shembe founds the Church of the Nazarenes (Ibandia lamaNazaretha, an important example of a Zionist, African-initiated prophetic church), building a community at Ekuphakameni. [**Africa: South Africa**]

1910 The quasi-religious Mexican Revolution under Emiliano Zapata and others leads to the end of a thirty-year dictatorship and to the establishment of a constitutional republic, but this revolution also contributes to further repression of the Catholic Church in Mexico. [**Latin America and the Caribbean: Mexico**]

1910 The World Missionary Conference begins in Edinburgh, attended by 1,215 invited delegates from European and American missionary societies, but only eighteen from the non-Western world; the Conference addresses the promotion of global mission under the slogan of "The Evangelization of the World in This Generation," and, despite its colonial paternalism, is significant as a direct ancestor of the ecumenical movement. [**Europe: United Kingdom of Great Britain and Northern Ireland (Scotland)**]

1910–1915 *The Fundamentals* (a set of ninety essays challenging theological liberalism and Biblical Criticism, published quarterly over a period of five years) defines the characteristic doctrines of what comes to be known as Fundamentalism; the gathering of six thousand conservative Christians for the first Conference of the World's Christian Fundamentals Association in Chicago in 1919 reinforces the impact of this series. [**North America: United States of America**]

1910s Republican anticlericalism in Cuba and Uruguay leads to the disestablishment of the Catholic Church in these countries. [**Latin America and the Caribbean: Cuba, Uruguay**]

1911 A Nationalist Revolution led by Huang Xing overthrows the Qing Dynasty, resulting in the declaration of the first Chinese republic under Christian President Sun Yat-Sen the following year. [**Asia: China**]

1912 Kalabari Anglican Garrick Sokari Braide receives a number of visionary experiences and assumes a prophetic role, eventually preaching to thousands of followers in the Niger delta as well as healing and baptizing his converts. [**Africa: Nigeria**]

1913 French Lutheran polymath Dr. Albert Schweitzer (philosopher, liberal theologian, and world-class organist) arrives in Lambaréné, Gabon as a medical missionary; while there, he conceives his ethical philosophy Ehrfurcht vor dem Leben (Veneration for Life) and later receives the Nobel Peace Prize for his hospital work, which exemplifies this philosophy, in 1952. [**Africa: Gabon**]

1913 Pentecostal mission work begins in Fiji with the arrival of missionaries Albert and Lou Page, although they are largely unsuccessful, the Assemblies of God not officially beginning in Fiji until 1926. [**Oceania: Fiji**]

1913 The Kikuyu controversy erupts in the Kenyan Anglican church following Anglican participation in an ecumenical communion at a missionary conference; Bishop Frank Weston sees their attendance as vitiating the traditional teaching and practice of the Church of England, and castigates it as schismatic and heretical. [**Africa: Kenya**]

1913 The Liberian Grebo prophet William Wade Harris begins preaching campaigns, becoming the most successful missionary ever in West Africa with one hundred thousand converts in little more than a year. [**Africa: Côte d'Ivoire, Ghana, Liberia**]

1913 The nationalist prophet John Chilembwe begins preaching in Nyasaland (Malawi) after the 1913 famine; this leads to an unsuccessful uprising against colonial rule after the outbreak of the First World War. [**Africa: Malawi**]

1914 A gathering of about three hundred preachers and laymen convenes in Hot Springs, Arkansas, to discuss the formation of a cooperative Pentecostal fellowship; this results in the incorporation of the Assemblies of God in the United States. [**North America: United States of America**]

1914 The assassination of the Austrian Archduke Franz Ferdinand and his wife Sophie in Sarajevo, Bosnia and Herzegovina, by nineteen-year-old Serbian nationalist Gavrilan Princip, ignites simmering tensions in the Balkans, triggers the competing alliances of the European

Great Powers (Germany, Austria-Hungary, Russia, France, and Great Britain), and unleashes the First World War in Europe. [**Europe: Bosnia and Herzegovina**]

1915 Baptist missionaries in Ngombe-Luteta, central Congo, baptize Simon Kimbangu, later to become the founder of an influential African prophetic movement. [**Africa: Democratic Republic of the Congo**]

1915 Colonial French authorities in Côte d'Ivoire, fearing that the spectacular successes of the Grebo prophet William Wade Harris in converting whole villages to Christianity would have political implications for both the government and the Catholic Church, expel him back to his homeland of Liberia. [**Africa: Côte d'Ivoire, Liberia**]

1915 White Protestant nativists in the state of Georgia revive and extend the antiblack Ku Klux Klan to become an anti-Catholic, anti-Jewish, and anti-Trade Union organization. [**North America: United States of America**]

1915–1918 The Ottoman government begins a massacre of nearly half of all Christian Armenians in Turkey (one million out of 2.2 million); historian Arnold Toynbee calls this pogrom "the organized murder of the Armenian race." [**Asia: Armenia, Turkey**]

1916 Armed Senussi Bedouin bandits murder the French hermit priest Charles de Foucauld in the Saharan oasis of Tamanrasset, but communities of his "Little Brothers of Jesus" continue to follow his teaching and practice after his death. [**Africa: Algeria**]

1916 The Kalabari prophet Garrick Sokari Braide reaches the pinnacle of his influence in the Niger Delta, becoming known to his followers as Elijah II. [**Africa: Nigeria**]

1916 The Ross Sea Party, under Captain Aeneas Mackintosh of Sir Ernest Shackleton's Imperial Transantarctic Expedition of 1914–1917, erects a cross at Cape Evans in memory of three party members who had died there. [**Antarctica**]

1917 A revolution in February results in the formation of a Russian Provisional Government and the abdication of the Tsar; in a second revolution eight months later, the Bolshevik Party led by Vladimir Ilyich Ulyanov (Lenin) establishes a Communist government that would eventually become the Soviet Union. [**Europe: Russian Federation**]

1917 Following the overthrow of Tsar Nicholas II and the collapse of Russian rule in Georgia, the Georgian bishops unilaterally restore the autocephalous Georgian patriarchate. [**Asia: Georgia**]

1917 Walter Rauschenbusch's *A Theology for the Social Gospel* provides a systematic basis for the diversified "Social Gospel" movement that had emerged in the second half of the nineteenth century; this movement emphasizes the Kingdom of God, applying Christian theology and ethics to the resolution of issues of social justice. [**North America: United States of America**]

1918 Māori faith healer Tahupōtiki Wiremu Rātana begins his ministry; this later leads to the founding of the Rātana Church, the creation of a long-term Rātana-Labour Party political alliance, and the gaining of several seats in Parliament. [**Oceania: New Zealand**]

1918 Simon Kimbangu begins receiving visions; several similar prophetic movements around the world also emerge following the influenza pandemic that year (e.g. T. W. Rātana in New Zealand). [**Africa: Democratic Republic of the Congo**]

1918 The adoption of the Constitution of the Russian Soviet Federated Socialist Republic severs the centuries-old relationship between the Orthodox Church and the Russian state, thereby removing the Church's legal position of privilege and power, denying its clergy the right to vote or to hold office in the state, and depriving them of the right to food rations and education for their children. [**Europe: Russian Federation**]

1918 The Aladura (Yoruba: "Owners of prayer") churches start as prayer groups within the older churches in Nigeria, expanding to become a widespread network of diverse groups throughout Africa. [**Africa: Nigeria**]

1919 Pope Benedict XV's Apostolic Letter *Maximum Illud* calls for a rejection of colonialist interests and for a greater emphasis on the training of indigenous clergy to take over from European missionaries in churches throughout the world; Pope Pius XI's encyclical *Rerum Ecclesiae* in 1926 reinforces Benedict's call, having a major impact on Catholic missions, particularly in Uganda. [**Africa: Uganda**]

1919 The March First Movement (an independence movement against Japanese rule) emerges in Korea, supported by many Christians; this reflects Korean resistance to Japanese imperialism. [**Asia: Republic of Korea (South Korea)**]

1920 Converted criminal Sampson Oppong preaches to the Asante people in Ghana in the early 1920s; a mass movement to Christianity follows, with the Methodists being particular beneficiaries of these conversions. [**Africa: Ghana**]

1920 Under the Treaty of Paris and as a result of strong Maronite pressure, Lebanon gains independence from Syria, coming under a French mandate in order to protect religious, ethnic, and regional differences within the region. [**Asia: Lebanon**]

1920s The American Methodist missionary and pioneer of contextualization E. Stanley Jones organizes the interreligious Round Table Conferences between Christians, Hindus, Sikhs, and Buddhists. [**Asia: India**]

1920s This decade marks the height of Euro-American missionary activity in China, with the thousands of missionaries during this period making it the largest mission field in the history of Christianity. [**Asia: China**]

1921 After eighteen years of mission work in Burkina Faso, French priest Johanny Thévenoud becomes Vicar Apostolic of Ouagadougou and, as such, combines missionary concern and farsighted practical social involvement; this helps to expand the Catholic Church and assist the national development of Burkina Faso. [**Africa: Burkina Faso**]

1921 Simon Kimbangu begins an influential African-initiated church, the "Church of Jesus Christ through the prophet Simon Kimbangu," but the Belgian authorities arrest him and sentence him to life imprisonment for undermining public security and disturbing the peace; despite his imprisonment, the Kimbanguist movement spreads. [**Africa: Democratic Republic of the Congo**]

1922 A small group of Indian Christians, led by an English Anglican missionary, Father Jack Winslow, sets up the first Christian Ashram, Christa Seva Sangha ("The Society of the Servants belonging to Christ"). [**Asia: India**]

1922 Ching Tien-Ying founds the communitarian Family of Jesus in Shantung, a kind of Chinese monasticism; this grows to three hundred communities by 1950. [**Asia: China**]

1922-1943 French Catholic Bishop François Xavier Vogt, Vicar Apostolic in Yaoundé, oversees a period of extraordinary Catholic growth in Cameroon through the impetus of large numbers of well-trained Ewondo catechists. [**Africa: Cameroon**]

1923 Two Christian and Missionary Alliance couples begin missionary work in Phnom Penh and Battambang, planting what eventually would become the Protestant Église Khmer Évangelique (Khmer Evangelical Church). [**Asia: Cambodia**]

1923-1924 Cardinal Juan Bautista Benlloch y Vivó, Archbishop of Burgos, tours South America urging Hispanidad (Spanishness), i.e. the rooting of Latin American identity in Spanish Catholicism. [**Latin America and the Caribbean**]

1924 Protestant missionaries arrive in Ivory Coast and begin to attract an influx of Christians previously converted under William Wade Harris, who had told his followers to await "teachers with Bibles." [**Africa: Côte d'Ivoire**]

1925 A majority of Chilean Catholics accept the State's decision to disestablish the Catholic Church under the Constitution of 1925. [**Latin America and the Caribbean: Chile**]

1925 Jesuit Bishop Henri de Lespinasse Saune ordains nine priests, the first diocesan clergy in Madagascar; one of these, Ignace Ramarosandratna, becomes the first Malagasy bishop and Apostolic Vicar in 1939. [**Africa: Madagascar**]

1925 Presbyterian missionaries achieve great success among the Bulu, a major Bantu ethnic group, with more than seventy thousand converts being baptized in 1925. [**Africa: Cameroon, Equatorial Guinea, Gabon**]

1925 The "Monkey Trial" begins in Dayton, Tennessee, with John Scopes, a young science teacher, being accused of teaching evolution in violation of Tennessee state law; although the court finds him guilty, the Fundamentalist case against him becomes a focus for public ridicule. [**North America: United States of America**]

1926 Chinese Christian Ni To-sheng (Watchman Nee) founds the radically independent and deinstitutionalized Xiao Qun ("Little Flock") Church; Nee attracts considerable attention in the West through his sermons and Bible studies, based on his magazine articles and on notes taken down by his students, and published after his arrest and imprisonment by the Communist authorities in 1952. [**Asia: China**]

1927 Methodist Christian Kawai Shinsui founds the Christ Heart Church as a syncretistic religious body, incorporating Shintōism, Buddhism, and Confucianism as well as Christianity. [**Asia: Japan**]

1927 Pope Pius XI ordains Januarius Kyunosake Hayasaka as Bishop of Nagasaki, the first native Catholic bishop in Japan; Hayasaka serves for ten years, before resigning and then becoming the titular bishop of Philomelium (Akşehir, Turkey) in 1937. [**Asia: Japan**]

1927 Soviet authorities release Metropolitan Sergii Stragorodskii from prison, whereupon he seeks to find accommodation with the state by issuing a declaration accepting its recognition of the Russian Orthodox Church; this declaration causes sharp dissent within the Orthodox Church, those still in prison for their resistance to the Government seeing it as a "sellout" to the atheistic state. [**Europe: Russian Federation**]

1927 Under the leadership of Canadian Anglican missionary bishop Charles H. Brent, more than four hundred delegates from the Anglican, Baptist, Congregationalist, Lutheran, Methodist, Presbyterian, and Quaker Churches met at Lausanne to form the Faith and Order Movement (together with the complementary Life and Work Movement) to examine the differences of belief, liturgical practice, polity, and ministry among the various Christian denominations with a view to understanding this diversity; these two movements are important precursors of the Ecumenical Movement. [**Europe: Switzerland**]

1928 New York Governor Alfred E. Smith stands in the 1928 election as the first Catholic candidate for the presidency of the United States, but suffers a landslide defeat against Herbert Hoover. [**North America: United States of America**]

1928 The Second World Missionary Conference convenes in Jerusalem, but its mood (in the aftermath of the first World War and the 1917 Communist Revolution) is much less triumphalist than that of the First Conference in Edinburgh eighteen years earlier. [**Asia: State of Palestine**]

1929 Following the end of the Cristero War (1927–1929), the incoming president, Emilio Cándido Portes Gil, lifts the restrictions against the Mexican church, although tensions between the church and the state continue until the 1940s. [**Latin America and the Caribbean: Mexico**]

1929 The Catholic White Fathers begin preaching to the Dagarti people in northwest Ghana, later receiving a highly receptive response after a dramatic answer to prayers for rain in July 1932. [**Africa: Ghana**]

1929 The Lateran Pacts between Pope Pius XI and the Italian dictator Benito Mussolini establish the Vatican City State as an independent political entity. [**Europe: Holy See (Vatican City)**]

1930 After ruling Ethiopia behind the scenes for a decade, Tafari Makonnen, the Ras (or duke) of Shewa, becomes the Emperor Haile Selassie and, as such, reforms and modernizes the country, ruling until the Marxist coup d'état in 1974; Haile Selassie is a central figure in the Jamaican "Rastafarian" religion, the name of which derives from his title Ras Tafari. [**Africa: Ethiopia**]

1930s Independent churches grow exponentially among the Shona in Zimbabwe, partly as a response to the economic and political dominance of the white settler community, and partly from the impact of the Depression. [**Africa: Zimbabwe**]

1933 Pope Pius XI appoints Jean Baptiste Nguyễn Bá Tòng as Bishop of Phát Diêm, thus making him the first indigenous Vietnamese bishop. [**Asia: Viet Nam**]

1934 Almost all of the Protestant groups in Madagascar amalgamate to form the "United Protestant Church of Madagascar," although this represents a collaborative association for mission, rather than a total merger. [**Africa: Madagascar**]

1934 Following the Synod of Barmen's theological declaration against Nazism in May 1934, the second Synod of Dahlem seven months later creates the Bekennende Kirche (Confessing Church) in opposition to the Nazi-dominated Reich Church. [**Europe: Germany**]

1935 Catholic missions in Rwanda and Burundi have considerable success, with a mass movement of Tutsi converts into the church; at the movement's peak, there are more than a thousand baptisms a week. [**Africa: Burundi, Rwanda, Uganda**]

1935 The Italian Duce Benito Mussolini launches an invasion of Ethiopia and subjects the country to annexation and military occupation; this results in the expulsion of non-Italian missionaries, the Italianization of the Ethiopian church and its detachment from its centuries-old relationship with the See of Alexandria, and the execution of its Abuna (the leader of the church). [**Africa: Ethiopia**]

1936 The Congregatio de Propaganda Fide accepts that Shinto rites are patriotic rather than religious in nature, thus permitting Japanese Catholics to attend these rites without fear of committing idolatry. [**Asia: Japan**]

1936-1938 The Soviet government launches the Stalinist Great Purge; estimates place the total number of people killed at between seven hundred thousand and 1.2 million, including many bishops and priests who are imprisoned and executed. [**Europe: Russian Federation**]

1938 Bernhard Lichtenburg, Provost of St. Hedwig's Cathedral in Berlin, bravely protests the arrest of more than twenty thousand Jews and the destruction of nearly two hundred synagogues on Kristallnacht ("The Night of Broken Glass") on November 9-10, 1938; he is the only priest in the entire German Reich to speak out against this violence: "We are witnesses of what is happening today. Outside [this church] a synagogue is burning—and a synagogue too, is a house of God." [**Europe: Germany**]

1938 The Third World Missionary Conference convenes in Tambaram, India, with representatives from the so-called "younger" (i.e. non-Western) churches being in the majority for the first time. [**Asia: India**]

1939 Germany invades Poland; as a consequence, Britain and France (who had guaranteed military support for Poland in the event of its being attacked) declare war on Germany, thus beginning the Second World War. [**Europe: Germany, Poland**]

1939 The Japanese Government passes a Religious Organizations Law, which enables it to close down, or at least to control, those religious organizations that it considers are counter to the state Shinto "imperial way," centered on veneration of the emperor as *arahitogami* (a god who is a human being) and symbol of Japanese national identity. [**Asia: Japan**]

1939 Ugandan prelate Joseph Kiwánuka becomes the Apostolic Vicar of Masaka and the titular bishop of Thibica (an obsolete see in modern Tunisia), and thus the first indigenous African Catholic bishop since 1520. [**Africa: Uganda**]

1940 Japanese Christian pacifist, reformer, and labor activist Toyohiko Kagawa makes an apology to the Republic of China for Japan's occupation of the country, resulting in his arrest and imprisonment by the Japanese authorities. [**Asia: Japan**]

1940 Swiss Protestant Roger Schütz founds the Taizé Community, an ecumenical religious order, in Taizé, Saône-et-Loire, France; the community includes more than one hundred brothers from many countries, and from both Catholic and Protestant traditions, and has, since its founding, become a significant site of Christian pilgrimage. [**Europe: France**]

ca.1940 The Catholic sannyāsi (a religious ascetic who renounces the world) Brahmachari Rewachand Animinanda founds the first Catholic Ashram in Ranchi, Jharkand. [**Asia: India**]

1941 The Japanese Government forces the founding of the Nippon Kirisuto Kyodan (United Church of Christ in Japan) and compels all Japanese Protestants to merge with it (although some groups refuse to comply); the new church acquiesces to Japanese culture, as dictated by the government. [**Asia: Japan**]

1943 George Bell, bishop of Chichester, condemns the saturation bombing of German cities such as Hamburg and Dresden, which had resulted in many deaths among their civilian populations. [**Europe: United Kingdom of Great Britain and Northern Ireland (England)**]

1945 Ahmad Sukarno and Mohammed Hatta issue the Proklamasi Kemerdekaan Indonesia (Proclamation of Indonesian Independence) from Dutch colonial rule; many Christians (e.g. Amir Sjarifuddin) back this movement. [**Asia: Indonesia**]

1945 The discovery of the Nag Hammadi manuscripts in Upper Egypt provides a catalyst for a major reevaluation of the nature of Gnosticism and of early Christian history. [**Africa: Egypt**]

1945–1947 The installation of one-party Communist governments in most Eastern European countries and in the Balkan States leads to the oppression of the churches there to varying degrees, the closure of churches and church schools, the imprisonment of thousands of clergy, and to the promotion of state atheism. [**Europe: Eastern Europe**]

1946 The "Statement of the National Christian Council for a Christian Movement for the Founding of a New Japan" confesses Japan's responsibility for the events of World War II and serves notice of Japanese Christians' intention to Christianize all of Japan. [**Asia: Japan**]

1946 The king of Rwanda, Mutara III Rudahigwa, converts to Catholicism in 1943 and ceremonially dedicates his country to Christ three years later, effectively making Christianity the state religion of Rwanda-Urundi (the name by which the territories of Rwanda and Burundi were then jointly known). [**Africa: Burundi, Rwanda**]

1947 After protracted negotiations, the Anglican, Presbyterian, Methodist, Congregationalist, and Reformed churches in South India and Sri Lanka unite to form the Church of South India. [**Asia: India**]

1947 Pentecostal evangelists William Branham and Oral Roberts both begin to conduct healing crusades, reaching a wide public audience previously not receptive to Pentecostalism. [**North America: United States of America**]

1947 The partition of the British Raj into two independent dominions (Hindu India and Moslem Pakistan) displaces more than fourteen million people along religious lines, creating overwhelming refugee crises in the new dominions. [**Asia: India, Pakistan**]

1947 US Navy Lieutenant Commander (and Catholic priest) William Menster conducts the first complete religious service in Antarctica, consecrating the continent to Christ during this tent service on the ice. [**Antarctica**]

1948 A Pentecostal awakening at the Sharon Orphanage and Schools in North Battleford, Saskatchewan, results in a radically independent "Latter Rain" movement that spreads worldwide, helping to lay the foundations for an expansion of independent Pentecostal groups in the 1950s and the emergence of the Charismatic Movement in the 1960s. [**North America: Canada**]

1948 Albanian nun Agnes Gonxha Bojaxhiu, later known as "Mother" Teresa, leaves the Sisters of Loreto in Calcutta to found the Missionaries of Charity as an order working directly with the poorest of the poor. [**Asia: India**]

1948 The British mandate over Palestine ends (in line with United Nations Resolution 181) on 14 May 1948 and David Ben-Gurion proclaims the establishment of the State of Israel, becoming its first Prime Minister. [**Asia: Israel**]

1948 The first Assembly of the World Council of Churches takes place in Amsterdam, with 147 churches from different confessions and many countries coming together to commit themselves to the ecumenical movement. [**Europe: Netherlands**]

1949 Billy Graham gains national media coverage for his Los Angeles crusade after the media magnate William Randolph Hearst orders his editors to "Puff Graham" (i.e. to make him front page news). [**North America: United States of America**]

1949 Following decades of conflict between the Nationalist Kuomintang under Chiang Kai-Shek and the Chinese Communist Party under Mao Zedong, the Communists come to power, ending the era of Western missions in China. [**Asia: China**]

1950 Hendrik Verwoerd's Apartheid ("Separate Development") regime utilizes Biblical models to maintain the uniqueness of peoples, thereby theoretically giving each distinct group the right to determine its own separate destiny. [**Africa: South Africa**]

1950 Pope Pius XII issues the bull *Munificentissimus Deus*, proclaiming the dogma of the Virgin Mary's bodily assumption into heaven as an article of Catholic faith on the basis of papal infallibility. [**Europe: Holy See (Vatican City)**]

1950 Under the Population Registration and Group Areas Acts, the South African authorities deport Colored (i.e. mixed race) Christian communities en masse from Cape Town to remote areas without churches. [**Africa: South Africa**]

1951 Following consultations between church leaders and government officials, Wu Yao-tsung (Y. T. Wu) draws up a Chinese Christian Manifesto, leading to the establishment of the Three-Self Patriotic Movement (TSPM). [**Asia: China**]

1953 The Zambian prophetess Alice Lenshina experiences visions and begins preaching, becoming the focus of a revival movement at the Lubwa mission, where she had been baptized. [**Africa: Zambia**]

A Timeline of Global Christianity

1954 Although the 1954 Constitution of the People's Republic of China guarantees religious freedom, the ruling Communist Party imposes the Three-Self Patriotic Movement on the churches as the sole politically acceptable Christian body in China. [**Asia: China**]

1954 The French withdraw completely from Viet Nam, resulting in the division of the country into the communist North and the republican South; churches in the North face numerous restrictions, leading many Christians to flee to the South. [**Asia: Viet Nam**]

1955 A Conference of Roman Catholic bishops in Latin America, the Consejo Episcopal Latinoamericano (Latin American Episcopal Council) or CELAM I, sets up a General Secretariat with the approval of the Vatican. [**Latin America and the Caribbean: Colombia**]

1955 Conflict between Christians and Muslims erupts in the Sudan and continues until 1972; this breaks out again in 1983 over the imposition of Shari'a law by President Nimeiri. [**Africa: Sudan**]

1955 Rosa Park's arrest in Montgomery, Alabama, for refusing to give up her seat in the colored section of the bus to a white passenger ignites the American Civil Rights movement. [**North America: United States of America**]

1955 Two years after the 1953 Lubwa revival, followers of the prophetess Alice Lenshina form the independent Lumpa Church, combining Christian and traditional African values but disallowing practices such as polygamy and idolatry; this church later becomes more radical, rejecting all secular authority and refusing to pay taxes, resulting in armed confrontations with the Zambian government in 1964. [**Africa: Zambia**]

1956 After working for thirteen years in Sophiatown, South Africa, as a much loved priest and vigorous anti-apartheid campaigner, English Anglican bishop Trevor Huddleston publishes his seminal book *Nought for Your Comfort*. [**Africa: South Africa**]

1956 President Ğamāl Abdel Nāsser nationalizes the Suez Canal, provoking the retaliatory invasion of the Egyptian Sinai by Israel, together with Britain and France; Nāsser also declares Islam the religion of the state, leading to an exodus of Coptic Christians. [**Africa: Egypt**]

1957 Kwame Nkrumah leads Ghana to self-government, later becoming the first African head of state to promote Pan-Africanism; this movement takes concrete form in the Organization of African Unity in Addis Ababa, Ethiopia in 1963, set up to consolidate the independence of the increasing number of post-colonial African states in the 1960s. [**Africa: Ghana**]

1958 A major schism emerges in the Kenyan church, resulting in the formation of the Church of Christ in Africa; members of this group oppose Revivalist emphases, but paradoxically name themselves Johera, "People of Love." [**Africa: Kenya**]

1958 Elderly Italian Cardinal Angelo Giuseppe Roncalli becomes Pope John XXIII; although expected to be a short-term "caretaker pope" and only reigning for five years, he launches the *aggiornimento* ("bringing up to date") of Canon Law and convenes the Second Vatican Council, which implements many of his concerns for reform. [**Europe: Holy See (Vatican City)**]

1958–1964 Premier Nikita Khrushchev launches an anti-religious campaign in the Soviet Union; this takes the form of mass closures of churches, monasteries, convents, and seminaries, the restriction of parental rights to teach religion to their children, a ban on the presence of children in Church services, and other restrictions on Church life. [**Europe: Russian Federation**]

1959 A highly successful Church Growth movement begins in Korea, leading to the doubling of Protestant church membership between 1957 and 1967; this parallels the beginning of rapid economic growth, which some scholars attribute as partly a product of the religious entrepreneurship of the 1960s. [**Asia: Republic of Korea (South Korea)**]

1959 After decades of opposition and persecution, the Belgian colonial government recognizes the Église de Jésus Christ sur la Terre par Son Envoyé Special Simon Kimbangu (Church of Jesus Christ on Earth by His Special Envoy Simon Kimbangu) as a legitimate church; ten years later, it becomes the first such Church to be received into the World Council of Churches, giving it an appreciated badge of acceptability. [**Africa: Democratic Republic of the Congo**]

1959 Cuba falls to communist revolutionaries led by Fidel Castro, becoming the first communist dictatorship in Latin America; the Party's insistence on Marxist-Leninist principles (including atheism), together with the rejection of Communism by the Cuban Catholic hierarchy, leads to discrimination and the severe restriction of religious practice in Cuba. [**Latin America and the Caribbean: Cuba**]

1959 Emperor Haile Selassie abolishes the Egyptian Coptic Church's traditional right of appointment of the Abuna (the head of the Ethiopian Church) and upgrades the Abuna's role to a full Patriarchate. [**Africa: Egypt, Ethiopia**]

1960 Archbishop Laurean Rugambwa of Das es Salaam, a Haya Catholic of royal descent, becomes the first African cardinal of modern times. [**Africa: United Republic of Tanzania**]

1960 Democratic nominee John F. Kennedy defeats Richard Nixon in the 1960 Presidential election to become the first Catholic President of the United States. [**North America: United States of America**]

1960 Episcopal priest Dennis Bennett announces his experience of the Baptism in the Spirit to his congregation at St. Mark's Episcopal Church in Van Nuys, California, thus launching the Protestant Charismatic Movement. [**North America: United States of America**]

1960 Joost de Blank, the Anglican archbishop of Cape Town, calls for the expulsion of the Nederduitse Gereformeerde Kerk (NGK, the Dutch Reformed Church in South Africa) from the World Council of Churches because of its support of apartheid. [**Africa: South Africa**]

1960 Many of independent Africa's new rulers come from Christian backgrounds; examples include Kwame Nkrumah (Ghana), who holds a Bachelor of Theology degree from his university study in the United States, Leopold Senghor (Senegal), Julius Nyerere (United Republic of Tanzania), and Kenneth Kaunda (Zambia). [**Africa: Ghana, Senegal, United Republic of Tanzania, Zambia**]

1960 The massacre of sixty-nine people (mainly women) in a crowd protesting against the Pass Laws at a police station in the township of Sharpeville galvanizes international opinion against apartheid. [**Africa: South Africa**]

1961 A Consultation of the Pacific Churches, held in Malua, Samoa, leads to the formation of a Pacific-wide Pacific Conference of Churches five years later; the Conference currently has twenty-seven member churches in seventeen island states and territories. [**Oceania: Samoa**]

1961 The World Council of Churches and eight South African member churches issue a declaration against the exclusion of believers from any church on the basis of color or race. [**Africa: South Africa**]

1961 Uruguayan Jesuit theologian Juan Luis Segundo begins teaching his Cursos de Complementación Cristiana ("Courses of Christian Complementation") in Montevideo, analyzing political, social, and economic problems in the light of the Catholic faith. [**Latin America and the Caribbean: Uruguay**]

1962 A series of apparitions to several Luo Roman Catholics of a mystic woman with messages about the incarnation of the Son of God as a black man leads to the founding of Legio Maria (Legion of Mary); although this is an independent African-initiated Catholic church, it does have some connections with earlier apparitions such as the Apparition of Fátima. [**Africa: Kenya**]

1962-1965 The Second Vatican Council convenes, with more than two thousand eight hundred bishops from 116 countries (together with thousands of observers and laypersons, both Catholic and Protestant) attending its four sessions between 1962 and 1965; church historians view the Council as one of the most significant religious events of the twentieth century, since it attempted take account of the world outside the Church and to remove the "fortress mentality" that had characterized Catholicism since Vatican I in 1870. [**Europe: Holy See (Vatican City)**]

1964 The growth of Alice Lenshina's Lumpa Church leads to a number of violent clashes (the "Lumpa Uprising") between her followers and Kenneth Kaunda's United National Independence Party, in which between seven hundred and fifteen hundred people lose their lives. [**Africa: Zambia**]

1964-1985 Hélder Camara, the archbishop of Olinda and Recife, speaks out against the Brazilian government as part of a clergy critique of the military regimes for neglecting justice and abusing human rights; in response, the government dispatches several assassination squads in an attempt to silence him. [**Latin America and the Caribbean: Brazil**]

1965 After the foiling of an attempted Communist coup d'état in Indonesia and the deaths of more than three hundred thousand people in the reprisals that followed, thousands of people flock to join Christian churches (partly in order to distance themselves from the atheism implicit in Communism). [**Asia: Indonesia**]

1965 Dictator Joseph-Désiré Mobutu places increasing restrictions on the churches, forcing their consolidation into three bodies: the United Church of Christ in Zaire, the Catholics, and the Kimbanguists. [**Africa: Democratic Republic of the Congo**]

1966 Michael Ramsay, the Archbishop of Canterbury, visits Pope Paul VI in Rome, the first such engagement of the leaders of the Anglican and Roman Catholic churches since the Reformation; following their meeting, they issue a Common Declaration, observing that this "marks a new stage in the development of fraternal relations, based upon Christian charity, and of sincere efforts to remove the causes of conflict and to reestablish unity." [**Europe: United Kingdom of Great Britain and Northern Ireland (England)**]

1966 Socialist Catholic priest Camilo Torres Restrepo leaves his academic post to join the revolutionary Ejército de Liberación Nacional (National Liberation Army) as a Marxist-Christian chaplain, but dies in his first guerrilla skirmish. [**Latin America and the Caribbean: Colombia**]

1966–1976 Chairman Mao Zedong unleashes the Cultural Revolution, his Red Guards closing all churches in China as part of a general campaign against religion, although many Christian groups go underground, continuing to spread in spite of harsh restrictions. [**Asia: China**]

1967 Enver Hoxha's hard-line Communist regime closes all religious institutions, bans all religious practices, and declares Albania to be the world's first and only "Atheist State"; this severe persecution virtually destroys the Albanian church. [**Europe: Albania**]

1967 The Catholic charismatic movement emerges at Duquesne University in Pittsburgh, later spreading to Notre Dame University in Indiana, and disseminating worldwide from these two locations. [**North America: United States of America**]

1968 A crucial meeting of Catholic bishops in Medellin (CELAM II), opened by Pope Paul VI during the first ever papal visit to Latin

America, declares that the Church will stand on the side of the poor. [**Latin America and the Caribbean: Colombia**]

1968 American astronauts Frank Borman, James Lovell, and Bill Anders beam back images of the Moon and Earth (including the famous "Earthrise" picture), and broadcast a reading of ten verses from Genesis 1 while orbiting the Moon in Apollo 8, closing with a Christmas wish for everyone "on the good earth." (**Moon: Lunar Orbit**)

1968 American fugitive and felon James Earl Ray assassinates Martin Luther King Jr., American Baptist minister and Nobel Prize-winning Civil Rights campaigner, on the balcony outside King's room at the Lorraine Motel in Memphis, Tennessee. [**North America: United States of America**]

1968 Francisco Macias Nguéma becomes the first president of Equatorial Guinea, but proves to be violently hostile to the Church, banning Christian funerals and Christian names, and declaring his country an "atheistical" state. [**Africa: Equatorial Guinea**]

1968 Renewal takes place in the Coptic Church following several apparitions of the Virgin Mary over a period of nearly a year at a church in Zeitoun, Cairo, leading to reports of miracles and healings (including among Muslims). [**Africa: Egypt**]

1968 The Methodist Church, the former LMS, and the more marginal Presbyterian Church amalgamate to become the United Church in Papua New Guinea and the Solomon Islands. [**Oceania: Papua New Guinea, Solomon Islands**]

1968 The papal encyclical *Humanae vitae*, affirming the Church's moral teaching on the sanctity of life (and also reiterating its ban on artificial methods of birth control), creates dissent in Catholic circles, with its opponents seeing it as abrogating efforts to limit population growth worldwide. [**Europe: Holy See (Vatican City)**]

1969 American astronaut Buzz Aldrin, an elder of the Webster Presbyterian church in Texas, celebrates communion on the Moon, using the elements of bread and wine from his church that he had brought with him on the Apollo 11 moon landing; although NASA covers up this "secret communion" due to legal pressure from militant atheist Madalyn Murray O'Hair, Aldrin's church still celebrates a "Lunar Communion Sunday" every July, using the chalice that he had brought back with him from the Moon. [(**Moon: Mare Tranquillitatis**); **North America: United States of America**]

1969 Pope Paul VI appoints Archbishop Stephen Kim Sou-hwan of Seoul as the first native Korean cardinal; as Cardinal, Kim boldly criticizes the "despotic" military dictatorship of South Korea for thirty years and advocates fearlessly (often as a lone voice) for democracy. [**Asia: Republic of Korea (South Korea)**]

1970 Churches in Pakistan and North India unite to form the Church of Pakistan and the Church of North India (incorporating the same groups as the Church of South India, but also including some smaller bodies). [**Asia: India, Pakistan**]

1970 Forty-six Protestant missions and churches combine to form the Église du Christ au Zaire (Church of Christ in Zaire); it now comprises sixty-two member denominations, making it the largest United Church in the world, ahead of the Evangelical Church in Germany. [**Africa: Democratic Republic of the Congo**]

1970 Korean theologian Ahn Byung Mu develops Minjung Sinhak (Minjung theology), a socio-theological emphasis on social justice; this is equivalent to, but not identical with, liberation theology in the Latin American context. [**Asia: Republic of Korea (South Korea)**]

1970 Marxist politician Salvador Guillermo Allende Gossens becomes the democratically elected president of Chile, but an authoritarian military coup d'état under General Augusto Pinochet overthrows him in 1973; Pinochet's régime then engages in the widespread imprisonment, torture, and killing of opponents. [**Latin America and the Caribbean: Chile**]

1970–1975 An exponential surge of Evangelical growth takes place in Cambodian churches over a five-year period as the ultra-Maoist Khmer Rouge tightens its siege cordons around major cities in Cambodia. [**Asia: Cambodia**]

1971 John Gatu, President of the Presbyterian Church of East Africa, calls for a Moratorium on Christian missionaries and funding from the West to enable the African church to develop their own mission identity; mission historians view Gatu's call as a symbolic milestone marking an end of the colonial paradigm and the beginning of the postcolonial mission era. [**Africa: Zambia**]

1971 Peruvian Dominican priest and theologian Gustavo Gutiérrez publishes his foundational text *Teología de la liberación (A Theology of Liberation)*, calling for Christian solidarity with the poor and oppressed, and emphasizing the duty of churches to aid them through civic and political involvement, and by changing existing institutions in order to promote social justice. **[Latin America and the Caribbean: Peru]**

1971 The Namibian struggle against the occupation of the country by South Africa and the imposition of apartheid (strongly led by the Christian churches, and channeled through the South West Africa People's Organization (SWAPO), the Namibian independence movement), takes a dramatic turn with the publication of a highly critical Open Letter on apartheid, followed by an at times heated four-hour encounter between Namibian Lutheran bishop Leonard Nangolo Auala and South African Prime Minister John Vorster. **[Africa: Namibia]**

1972 Filipino President Ferdinand Marcos issues Proclamation 1081 declaring Batas Militar sa Pilipinas (Martial Law in the Philippines); many churches, especially the Catholic Church, speak out against it, protesting the poverty and corruption that characterize his regime. **[Asia: Philippines]**

1972 Korean Christians identify themselves as "sending churches," founding the Korean Foreign Mission Association to facilitate mission outside Korea, and sending out its first twenty-four missionaries two years later; this number had grown to 27,436 missionaries by 2014. **[Asia: Republic of Korea (South Korea)]**

1972 President Mobutu orders the changing of Christian names to "authentic" African ones, bans all religious broadcasting, publications, and church youth groups, and nationalizes the Catholic University. **[Africa: Democratic Republic of the Congo]**

1974 Black and white Dutch Reformed ministers form the Broederkring ("Circle of Brothers") to resist apartheid within the South African Dutch Reformed churches; this becomes an important ecumenical center of opposition to apartheid. **[Africa: South Africa]**

1974 The Dergue, a Marxist military junta, overthrows Haile Selassie, the last Christian Emperor of Ethiopia, deposes Patriarch Abuna Tewophilos as head of the Ethiopian Orthodox Church and begins a regime marked by terror and opposition to Christianity. [**Africa: Ethiopia**]

1974-1984 The Argentine military suppresses a left wing insurgency, but the Catholic hierarchy, through its support for anachronistic social systems, fails to immediately condemn government terrorism in Argentina, as well as in Paraguay and Guatemala. [**Latin America and the Caribbean: Argentina, Guatemala, Paraguay**]

1975 Cambodia falls to the Khmer Rouge; under their regime, 25 percent of the population of six million and 90 percent of all Cambodian Christians are starved, tortured, executed, and worked to death as slave labor over the next four years. [**Asia: Cambodia**]

1976 A group of twenty-two theologians from Asia, Africa, and Latin America gather in Dar es Salaam to form the Ecumenical Association of Third World Theologians (EATWOT); this theological association seeks to facilitate the development of contextual and liberationist theological dialogue within grassroots and local communities. [**Africa: United Republic of Tanzania**]

1976 Following the worldwide changes resulting from Vatican II, Catholic-Protestant relations in the Pacific become more fraternal and Catholic bishops join the Pacific Conference of Churches. [**Oceania**]

1976 Pope Paul VI appoints Archbishop Jaime Lachica Sin of Manila as a cardinal; his title and surname lead to a widespread point of humor, in the Philippines and elsewhere, of his being the "Eighth cardinal (i.e. 'deadly') sin." [**Asia: Philippines**]

1977 Steve Biko, the honorary president of the Black People's Convention and founder of the Black Consciousness movement, dies violently while in in police custody, becoming a symbolic "martyr" for the anti-apartheid movement. [**Africa: South Africa**]

1978 After thirteen years of international isolation under a white minority government following its Unilateral Declaration of Independence from Britain, Southern Rhodesia begins a transition to black majority rule, the first Prime Minister of the new Zimbabwe Rhodesia being United Methodist Bishop and national leader Abel Tendekayi Muzorewa. [**Africa: Zimbabwe**]

1978 The College of Cardinals elects Polish Cardinal Karol Wojtyla as the first non-Italian pope for more than four hundred and fifty years;

as Pope John Paul II, he becomes a significant influence in the fall of communism in Eastern Europe, especially in Poland. [**Europe: Poland**]

1979 American televangelist Jerry Falwell forms the Moral Majority (a religiously conservative pressure group), marking the emergence of the "New Christian Right" as a significant religio-political force in the United States. [**North America: United States of America**]

1979 Mother Teresa wins the Nobel Peace Prize for her work with the destitute and the dying in Calcutta since 1948; as part of this work her sisterhood, the Missionaries of Charity, had built a network of homes for orphans, nursing homes for lepers, and hospices for the terminally ill in Calcutta, and also engaged in aid work in other parts of the world. [**Asia: India**]

1979 Pope John Paul II condemns the excesses of liberation theology in his address to the third general conference of the Latin American Catholic bishops (CELAM III), held at Puebla, Mexico. [**Latin America and the Caribbean: Mexico**]

1979 The Chinese government officially reopens the Ningbo Centennial Church, the first congregation of the Three-Self Churches in China to be restored for public worship after the Cultural Revolution. [**Asia: China**]

1979–1990 The Sandinista uprising leads to the formation of a Marxist regime in Nicaragua (despite the attempts of the CIA-backed Contras militia to overthrow this); the uprising provides the context and the impetus for a liberationist Nicaraguan "Church of the People." [**Latin America and the Caribbean: Nicaragua**]

1980 An assassin shoots Óscar Arnulfo Romero y Galdámez, the archbishop of San Salvador and a zealous campaigner for social justice, at the altar during his celebration of Mass in a hospital chapel. [**Latin America and the Caribbean: El Salvador**]

1980 Chinese churches set up the China Christian Council as an umbrella group for all Protestant churches; effectively this is a postdenominational body, since there had been no denominational structures in China since the suppression of Christianity in the 1950s. [**Asia: China**]

1980s A number of Marian apparitions occur during the decade in Kibého, Rwanda (1981 on), Nsimalen, Cameroon (1986), and Nairobi, Kenya (late 1980s); these are viewed as prophetic and miraculous events, with the Kibého apparition being interpreted as a forewarning of the 1994 Rwandan genocide. [**Africa: Cameroon, Kenya, Rwanda**]

1980s Dalit theology emerges among the lowest castes; this shares themes with Latin American liberation theology and promotes a Dalit self-identity as a people undergoing Exodus from oppressive sociopolitical systems. [**Asia: India**]

1981 President Anwār al-Sādāt effectively outlaws the Coptic Church, arresting Patriarch Shenouda III and a number of other bishops and priests (who Sādāt had accused of having political ambitions and of fostering sectarianism); however, this persecution is short-lived, as an assassin kills Sādāt a month later. [**Africa: Egypt**]

1982 Allan Boesak and the Nederduitse Gereformeerde Sendingkerk (NGS, the Dutch Reformed Mission Church, i.e. the black wing of the Dutch Reformed Church) persuade the World Alliance of Reformed Churches to suspend the Dutch Reformed Church for its support of apartheid. [**Africa: South Africa**]

1983 Catholic authorities remove Emmanuel Milingo, archbishop of Lusaka, from his see after criticism of his incorporation of African traditions of healing and exorcism into his ministry. [**Africa: Zambia**]

1984 Desmond Tutu, Anglican bishop of Lesotho and the first black Secretary-General of the South African Council of Churches, receives the 1984 Nobel Peace Prize for his opposition to apartheid; this award transforms the South African anti-apartheid struggle into an international movement. [**Africa: Lesotho, South Africa**]

1984 Pope John Paul II canonizes 103 Korean martyrs en masse in Seoul in the first ever canonization ceremony performed outside Rome; this is also the greatest number of beatifications in a single ceremony. [**Asia: Republic of Korea (South Korea)**]

1984 Pope John Paul II takes issue with liberation theology in his *Instruction on certain aspects of the "theology of liberation"* and reiterates his opposition during his papal visit to Lima the following year. [**Latin America and the Caribbean: Peru**]

1985 The Institute for Contextual Theology issues the Kairos document, sharply criticizing the South African apartheid regime, and advocating a "preferential option for the poor" and the kairos of reconciliation. [**Africa: South Africa**]

1986 Corazon Aquino wins the Filipino presidential election, but the national assembly declares incumbent Ferdinand Marcos the winner; this produces widespread nonviolent public protest, led by the churches and by Cardinal Sin, with nuns in full habits and carrying rosaries being prominent at the barricades. [**Asia: Philippines**]

1986 El Salvador's Christian Democrat administration, under CIA-backed José Napoleón Duarte, declares its reluctance to accept earthquake relief from Catholic agencies, due to the clergy's alleged support of the leftist insurgency over the past six years; some of Duarte's generals also refuse to permit the Red Cross to deliver humanitarian aid to civilian victims of El Salvador's civil war. [**Latin America and the Caribbean: El Salvador**]

1986 Nobel Peace Prize-winning anti-apartheid and human rights activist Desmond Tutu becomes the first black Anglican archbishop of Cape Town; he also becomes the president of the ecumenical All Africa Conference of Churches the same year, and after the end of apartheid, chairs the Truth and Reconciliation Commission, set up to investigate past human rights abuses, in 1994. [**Africa: South Africa**]

1987–1988 The exposure of financial and sexual scandals in the television evangelism industry (often dubbed "televangelism") demonstrates the wide public dissemination of this form of evangelical media and highlights the lack of regulation within the industry. [**North America: United States of America**]

1988 South African police, on the orders of the apartheid regime, burn down the Catholic Bishops' Conference building in Pretoria and blow up the headquarters of the South African Council of Churches in Johannesburg. [**Africa: South Africa**]

1989 Barbara Harris becomes Suffragan (or subordinate) Bishop of the Episcopal Diocese of Massachusetts and as such, the first ordained woman bishop in the Anglican Communion; the following year, Penny Jamieson extends the role of women leaders, becoming a full

Diocesan Bishop in Dunedin, New Zealand. [**North America: United States of America; Oceania: New Zealand**]

1989 Communism collapses in Eastern Europe with the holding of free democratic elections in Poland and Czechoslovakia, the opening of the borders with the West by Hungary and East Germany, and the removal of longtime Communist leaders in Bulgaria and Romania; the most symbolic moment is the dismantling of the Berlin Wall, which had kept East and West Berlin physically divided for twenty-eight years. [**Europe: Bulgaria, Czechia (Czech Republic), Germany, Hungary, Poland, Romania, Slovakia**]

1989 Four Catholic, Anglican, and Presbyterian church leaders in Mozambique, with encouragement from the political leaders of other African countries, mediate between the government and the rebel Resistência Nacional Moçambicana (RENAMO), the Mozambique National Resistance. [**Africa: Mozambique**]

1989 Frederick Willem de Klerk becomes president of South Africa and begins the unilateral dismantling of the structure of apartheid; the following year, the South African white minority Parliament votes to end the segregation of public facilities. [**Africa: South Africa**]

1989 In Poland, the Catholic Church becomes a focal point of anti-Communist activism and its pressure for reform a powerful element in the emergence of the Solidarity movement; this develops into a mass campaign for political change, winning a majority in the Polish elections and inspiring popular resistance to Communist regimes in Eastern Europe later that year. [**Europe: Poland**]

1989 Kong Hee founds a Pentecostal megachurch (City Harvest Church), espousing a materialist American-style Prosperity Gospel, and building a massive ultramodern multistory church building in Jurong West. [**Asia: Singapore**]

1989 Protesting students set up a series of democracy demonstrations in Tiananmen Square, Beijing, but the Chinese authorities brutally crush these, killing at least two hundred to three hundred students and other demonstrators; pictures of "Tank Man" (an unidentified and unarmed Chinese man standing in the path of a column of tanks, temporarily blocking their advance into the Square) become some of the most iconic media images of all time. [**Asia: China**]

1989 Soviet premier Mikhail Gorbachev visits Pope John Paul II at the Vatican; the two leaders agree to establish diplomatic relations and Gorbachev promises to allow greater religious freedom within the Soviet Union. [**Europe: Holy See (Vatican City)**]

1989 The Spanish Jesuit liberation theologian Jon Sobrino narrowly escapes a military assassination squad that kills six of his fellow Jesuits for their opposition to the El Salvadorian Civil War. [**Latin America and the Caribbean: El Salvador**]

1990 A National Conference of Church Leaders issues the Rustenburg Declaration, confessing its guilt and complicity in apartheid and calling for complete confession, forgiveness, and restitution. [**Africa: South Africa**]

1990 An anti-Armenian pogrom in Baku leads to the torture and killing of Christians (many of whom are burnt to death), and the destruction of the Armenian Church of St. Gregory the Illuminator. [**Asia: Azerbaijan**]

1990 Catholicism becomes legal again in Cambodia after its restriction under the Lon Nol regime from 1970 to 1975, its ruthless suppression under the Pol Pot Khmer Rouge regime from 1975 to 1979, and police harassment under the Vietnamese occupation from 1979 on. [**Asia: Cambodia**]

1990 During the annual May Day parade celebrating the end of World War II, Russian Christians participate in demonstrations against the Kremlin rulers in Red Square, Moscow; in the course of these demonstrations an Orthodox priest with a life-sized crucifix addresses Premier Gorbachev: "Christ is risen, Mikhail Sergeyevich." [**Europe: Russian Federation**]

1990 Pope John Paul II consecrates the new Basilica of Our Lady of Peace (believed by the *Guinness Book of Records* to be the largest church building in the world, although other sources dispute this claim) in Yamasoukro, the birthplace of the Côte d'Ivoire president Félix Houphouët-Boigny, who had just gifted the Basilica to the Catholic Church. [**Africa: Côte d'Ivoire**]

1990 President de Klerk legalizes the previously banned African National Congress, and releases Nelson Mandela from prison after twenty-seven years of imprisonment. [**Africa: South Africa**]

A Timeline of Global Christianity

1990s A number of secularist plurinational indigenous civil rights movements, based on *laicidad* (laicism: the independence of the state from church interference), emerge in Latin America, e.g. the Movimiento de Unidad Plurinacional Pachakutik—Nuevo Pais (Movement of Plurinational Unity Pachakutik—New Country) in Ecuador in 1995, and the Movimiento al Socialismo—Instrumento Político por la Soberanía de los Pueblos (Movement for Socialism—Political Instrument for the Sovereignty of the Peoples) in Bolivia in 1998; the latter becomes the government in the 2005 Bolivian elections. [**Latin America and the Caribbean: Ecuador, Plurinational State of Bolivia**]

1991 A coalition of ethnic-based parties overthrows the Marxist leader Mengistu Haile Mariam and reinstates the Coptic Orthodox church as the national religion of Ethiopia. [**Africa: Ethiopia**]

1991 After defeating long-serving President Kenneth Kaunda's United National Independence Party by a landslide majority in a snap election, Zambia's incoming president Frederick Chiluba officially declares the country to be a Christian nation. [**Africa: Zambia**]

1992 The Paraguayan Constitution recognizes the pervasiveness of Guaraní (the indigenous language spoken by the majority of the population), giving it equal footing with Spanish as a national language; its survival since the Spanish conquests of the sixteenth century is partly due to the fostering of the language in the Jesuit mission communities (*reducciónes* or "Reductions") which had safeguarded the Guaraní Indians from colonial oppression and enslavement. [**Latin America and the Caribbean: Paraguay**]

1994 After a sweeping 63 percent victory by his African National Congress party in the 1994 General Election, Nelson Mandela becomes the president of South Africa as the country's first black head of state, heading a multiparty Government of National Unity (which includes some of his political opponents). [**Africa: South Africa**]

1994 The controversial "Toronto Blessing" phenomenon emerges at the Toronto Airport Vineyard Christian Fellowship and rapidly spreads, creating a global Pentecostal pilgrimage industry. [**North America: Canada**]

1997 Mother Teresa dies in Calcutta; six years later Pope John Paul II beatifies her in the first step toward her canonization. [**Asia: India**]

1997 The Cambodian Catholic Church produces a Khmer translation of the Bible, but this unfortunately is not well received, being described as "shallow" and as "steamed white rice," in contrast to the "hearty oriental chicken dinner" of the original 1953 Hammond literal translation. [**Asia: Cambodia**]

1999 Ethnic religio-political violence erupts between Muslims and Christians in the Moluccas and Sulawesi (Celebes), including a campaign by the Laskar Jihād militia group to forcibly convert or else drive out Christians in the Moluccas. [**Asia: Indonesia**]

2001 Al-Qaeda hijackers carry out the September 11 attacks (known as "9/11") on the World Trade Centre, New York and the Pentagon in Washington DC; these terrorist attacks, the deadliest in history with almost three thousand deaths, lead to President George W. Bush's declaration of a "War on Terror" and the subsequent American-led invasions of Afghanistan and Iraq. [**North America: United States of America**]

2003 The government issues a Declaration of Religious Harmony in response to tensions following the 9/11 attacks in America and the arrest of members of the Jemaah Islamiyah terrorist network in Singapore. [**Asia: Singapore**]

2005 A study by the Pew Forum on Religion and Public Life locates the current center of gravity of world Christianity in Mali, reflecting its movement toward the global South.[4] [**Africa: Mali**]

2010 Singapore authorities investigate Pastor Kong Hee and sixteen other individuals in the megachurch Singapore City Harvest Church over misuse of church funds; six of these are arrested in 2012 and charged with breach of trust. [**Asia: Singapore**]

2012 Ellinah Ntombi Wamukoya, chaplain of the University of Swaziland, succeeds Meshack Mabuza as Anglican bishop of Swaziland, thus becoming the first woman bishop in Africa. [**Africa: Eswatini (Swaziland)**]

2013 The papal Conclave, convened to elect a successor to Pope Benedict XVI following his resignation (the first such papal renunciation since that of Gregory XII in 1415), elects the Argentinian Cardinal Jorge Mario Bergoglio of Buenos Aires as Pope Francis I; Francis's accession

---

4. Johnson, "Christianity in Global Context," 1.

also creates numerous firsts, since he is the first Latin American and Southern Hemisphere pope, the first Jesuit pope, and the first non-European pope since the Syrian Pope Gregory III in 741. [**Latin America and the Caribbean: Argentina**]

2013 Theodore Zurenuoc, the Speaker of the Papua New Guinea Parliament and a devout Christian, creates controversy by removing totems and nineteen traditional carvings from the Parliament building to cleanse it of evil spirits. [**Oceania: Papua New Guinea**]

2014 The Islamic extremist group Boko Haram kidnaps more than two hundred Christian schoolgirls from a Government Secondary School in Chibok and enslaves them, compelling them to convert to Islam, and forcing them into arranged marriages. [**Africa: Nigeria**]

2014–2016 "Europe's young adults and religion," a report based on the 2014–2016 European Social Survey, finds that a majority of young adults aged sixteen to twenty-nine years old in twenty-two European countries have no religious faith (Czechia, Estonia, and Sweden being the most irreligious at 91 percent, 80 percent, and 75 percent, respectively); by contrast, Poland has the highest religious adherence at 83 percent, followed by 75 percent for Lithuania. [**Europe: Czechia (Czech Republic), Estonia, Lithuania, Poland, Sweden**]

2015 A major refugee crisis emerges in Europe; by the end of 2016, nearly 5.2 million refugees had arrived across the Mediterranean from Syria, Iraq, Afghanistan, and Africa, and many thousands more had lost their lives or gone missing while attempting to reach safety. [**Europe: France, Greece, Italy**]

2016 Pope Francis I proclaims the canonization of Mother Teresa as Saint Teresa of Calcutta. [**Asia: India**]

2020 The Australian High Court overturns Australian Cardinal George Pell's conviction on historical child sexual abuse charges, releasing him from prison after having served thirteen months of a six-year sentence. [**Oceania: Australia**]

Continent and Country Index

This index lists entries from all six inhabited continents (and from Antarctica and Outer Space), as well as an additional category for the Greco-Roman world (which overlapped parts of the continents of Europe, Asia, and Africa up to 565). Each country in the list is referenced to the date(s) under which it appears in the main list and is also subsumed within a continental categorization, derived from the United Nations Statistics Division (UNSD) website;[5] those territories not listed in the website are enclosed in rounded brackets, e.g. (Ceuta), (Taiwan), (Tibet), etc. Entries relating to Christianity in outer space are also enclosed in rounded brackets, e.g. (Moon: Lunar Orbit) and (Moon: Mare Tranquillitatis). Greenland, although included in the North American continent in the UNSD website, was historically seen as being part of Europe (i.e. a Norwegian or Danish colony) and is so treated here.

5. United Nations Statistics Division, "Methodology."

Continent and Country Index

CONTINENT, COUNTRY, AND DATE

AFRICA

Algeria: 665–689, 1114, 1838, 1868, 1916
Angola: 1483, 1491, 1520, 1534, 1540, 1543, 1553, 1568, 1571, 1596, 1645, 1665, 1686, 1700s, 1853–1856, 1856, 1905
Benin: 1515, 1644, 1835, 1838, 1843
Botswana: 1847, ca.1860
Burkina Faso: 1901, 1921
Burundi: 1935, 1946
Cameroon: 1922–1943, 1925, 1980s
(Canary Islands): 1435
Cabo Verde: 1416, 1530s, 1604
(Ceuta): 1415
Congo: 1483, 1491, 1520, 1534, 1540, 1543, 1553, 1568, 1596, 1645, 1665, 1700s, 1878
Congo, Democratic Republic of the: 1483, 1491, 1520, 1534, 1540, 1543, 1553, 1568, 1596, 1645, 1665, 1700s, 1853–1856, 1878, 1885, 1886, 1893, 1905, 1915, 1918, 1921, 1959, 1965, 1970, 1972
Côte d'Ivoire: 1913, 1915, 1924, 1990
Djibouti: 1337
Egypt: 452–457, 640–670, 969–1171, 1009–1016, 1219, 1250, 1279, 1439, 1517, 1895, 1910, 1945, 1956, 1959, 1968, 1981
Equatorial Guinea: 1925, 1968
Eritrea: Before 356, Before 480, 520, ca.1860
Eswatini (Swaziland): 2012
Ethiopia: Before 356, Before 480, 520, 1337, 1436, 1494, 1531–1543, 1622, 1632, 1830s, 1839, 1842, 1846, 1855, 1878, 1880s, 1892, 1896, 1930, 1935, 1959, 1974, 1991
Gabon: 1842, 1913, 1925
Gambia: 1416
Ghana: 1482, 1742, 1752, 1765, 1787, 1828, 1838, 1913, 1920, 1929, 1957, 1960
Guinea: 1416, 1772
Guinea-Bissau: 1416
Kenya: 1844, 1913, 1958, 1962, 1980s
Lesotho: 1833, 1984
Liberia: 1822, 1847, 1913, 1915
Libya: 640–670, 1710–1711
Madagascar: 1820, 1835–1861, 1857, 1861, 1868, 1868, 1925, 1934
Malawi: 1853–1856, 1858, 1864, 1893, 1913
Mali: 2005
Mauritania: 1416
Mauritius: 1841–1842, 1857
Morocco: 665–689, 1220, 1432
Mozambique: 1853–1856, 1856, 1989
Namibia: 1811, 1971
Niger: 1710–1711
Nigeria: 1570s, 1710–1711, 1789, 1838, 1841, 1843, 1846, 1857, 1864, 1912, 1916, 1918, 2014
Réunion: 1841–1842, 1857
Rwanda: 1900, 1935, 1946, 1980s
Sao Tome and Principe: 1530s, 1534
Senegal: 1416, 1819, 1960
Sierra Leone: 1416, 1787, 1792, 1807, 1861, 1864
(Somaliland): 1337
South Africa: 1652, 1738, 1792, 1799, 1806, 1810, 1811, 1816, 1817, 1820, 1829, 1834–1835, 1835–1840, 1841, 1847, 1857, 1857, 1863, 1883, 1892, 1903, 1910, 1950, 1950, 1956, 1960, 1960, 1961, 1974, 1977, 1982, 1984, 1985, 1986, 1988, 1989, 1990, 1990, 1994
South Sudan: 1898
Sudan: 543, 569, 580, 640–670, By 701, 739, 836, 1272, 1315, 1317, 1500, 1742, 1846, 1898, 1955
Tanzania, United Republic of: 1844, 1853–1856, 1864, 1871, 1908, 1960, 1960, 1976
Togo: 1644, 1838, 1843
Tunisia: 665–689, 1076, 1176, 1293, 1884

Continent and Country Index

Uganda: 1874, 1877, 1879, 1886, 1890, 1893, 1919, 1935, 1939
Western Sahara: 1416, 1434
Zambia: 1853–1856, 1856, 1873, 1905, 1953, 1955, 1960, 1964, 1971, 1983, 1991
Zimbabwe: 1531, 1853–1856, 1856, 1930s, 1978

ANTARCTICA

Antarctica: 1916, 1947

ASIA

Afghanistan: 196, 497–498
Armenia: 288, 1894–1896, 1915–1918
Azerbaijan: 1275, 1990
Bahrain: 5th and 6th centuries, 410
Cambodia: 1923, 1970–1975, 1975, 1990, 1997
China: 497–498, 578, Early 630s, 635, 638, 698, 781, 840–846, 851, 878, 907, 987, 1206, 1265–1266, 1275, 1275, 1289, 1318, 1368, 1552, 1582, 1582, 1600, 1603, 1603, 1623, 1636, 1656, 1693, 1724, 1742, 1800, 1807, 1816, 1834, 1839–1842, 1844, 1850–1864, 1865, 1883, 1899–1901, 1903–1907, 1911, 1920s, 1922, 1926, 1949, 1951, 1954, 1966–1976, 1979, 1980, 1989
Georgia: ca.330, 1917
India: 52, ca.180–190, 345, 497–498, ca.542–578, 555, 1498, 1542, 1599, 1605, 1653, 1706, 1750, 1757, 1777, 1784, 1793, 1805, 1806, 1813, 1813, 1818, 1829, 1857–1858, 1885, 1920s, 1922, 1938, ca.1940, 1947, 1947, 1948, 1970, 1979, 1980s, 1997, 2016
Indonesia: ca.1300, 1318, 1346, 1534, 1537, 1546–1547, 1555, 1596, 1605, 1815, 1820, 1833, 1862, 1945, 1965, 1999

Iran (Persia), Islamic Republic of: 225, 340–363, 410, 424, 486, 540, ca.542–578, 569–571, 1287, 1318, 1834
Iraq: 104, ca.170, 225, 340–363, 5th and 6th centuries, 410, 424, 486, 540, ca.542–578, 569–571, 750, 779, 781, 1258, 1281
Israel: 1948
Japan: 735, 1549, 1579, 1587, 1597, 1598, 1600, 1601, 1614, 1616, 1622, 1637, 1639, 1854, 1865, 1865, 1873, 1880s, 1905, 1927, 1927, 1936, 1939, 1940, 1941, 1946
Kazakhstan: 497–498, 1206
Korea, Democratic Peoples' Republic of (North Korea): 1592, 1865, 1866–1867, 1876, 1882, 1883, 1890, 1894–1895, 1903–1907
Korea, Republic of (South Korea): 1592, 1783, 1789–1790, 1801, 1839, 1846, 1866–1867, 1882, 1890, 1894–1895, 1919, 1959, 1969, 1970, 1972, 1984
Kyrgyzstan: 497–498, 751
Lao People's Democratic Republic (Laos): 1642, 1858, 1876
Lebanon: 1860, 1900, 1920
Malaysia: 657, 1510, 1511, 1545, 1596, 1629
Mongolia: 1009, 1145, 1206, 1245–1247, 1252
Myanmar (Burma): ca.1000, 1510, 1554, 1813, 1817, 1824–1826, 1826, 1827, 1835, 1853, 1856, 1856, 1857, 1885
Oman: 5th and 6th centuries
Pakistan: 196, 497–498, 1947, 1970
Palestine, State of: 638, 1009–1016, 1099, 1187, 1244, 1260, 1928
Philippines: 1521, 1565, 1571, 1601, 1621, 1768, 1872, 1899, 1900, 1902, 1972, 1976, 1986
Qatar: 225, 5th and 6th centuries, 410
Russian Federation (Siberia: east of the Urals): 1850

Saudi Arabia: 373, 5th and 6th centuries, 610, 622
Singapore: 1819, 1851, 1989, 2003, 2010
Sri Lanka: 555, 1543, 1658, 1814, 1849, 1873
Syrian Arab Republic: 373, 1009–1016, 1860
(Taiwan): 1626, 1662
Tajikistan: 196, 497–498
Thailand: 1510, 1567, 1655–1709, 1664, 1817, 1835, 1851, 1870, 1875, 1893
(Tibet): 781, 1624, 1716
Timor-Leste: 1555, 1596
(Turkestan: Central Asia): 551, 591, Early 630s
Turkey: 489, 1054, 1071, 1204, 1261, 1453, 1894–1896, 1915–1918
Turkmenistan: 497–498
Uzbekistan: 196, 497–498, By 1370
Viet Nam: 1624, 1664, 1789, 1802–1810, 1821–1841, 1843, 1933, 1954
Yemen: 356, 5th and 6th centuries, 520, 555

EUROPE

Albania: 1967
Austria: 687, 751, 814, 1206, 1526–1529
Belarus: 957, 988, 1206
Belgium: 496, 687, 690, 751, 814
Bosnia and Herzegovina: 1219, 1557, 1879, 1914
Bulgaria: 864, 1989
Croatia: 1219, 1557, 1879
Czechia (Czech Republic): 814, 863, 1414, 1618, 1989, 2014–2016
Denmark: 829, 948, 1022, 1026, 1123, 1843
Estonia: 1242, 2014–2016
Europe (no further differentiation): 1346–1349
Europe, Eastern (no further differentiation): 1945–1947
Faroe Islands: 995
Finland: 1155, 1291

France: 496, 590, ca.590, 687, 732, 751, 779, 814, 910, 911, 1084, 1095, 1146, ca.1157, 1179, 1287, 1305–1377, 1378, 1559, 1572, 1598, 1682, 1685, 1703, 1789, 1841–1842, 1905, 1940, 2015
Germany: 341, ca.590, 687, 716, 751, 781, 814, 857, 955, 962, 1046, 1122, 1147, 1378, 1414, 1414–1418, 1450s, 1517, 1521, 1524–1525, 1525, 1529, 1534–1535, 1541, 1555, 1620, 1648, 1675, 1694, 1722, 1799, 1848, 1934, 1938, 1939, 1989
Greece: 1852, 2015
Greenland: 995, 1123
Holy See (Vatican City): 1929, 1950, 1958, 1962–1965, 1968, 1989
Hungary: 955, 975, 1206, 1526–1529, 1989
Iceland: 870, 995, 1004, 1016
Ireland: 432, ca.590, 851, 1696
Italy: 529, ca.530, 590, ca.590, 716, 800, 814, 867, 1049, 1054, 1059, 1075, 1076–1077, 1088, 1098, 1198–1216, 1210, 1215, 1216, 1232, 1274, 1287, 1302, 1378, 1378, 1431–1449, 1498, 1506, 1540, 1545–1563, 1610, 1622, 1740, 1773, 1854, 1868, 1891, 2015
Latvia: 1195
Liechtenstein: 687, 751, 814
Lithuania: ca.1251, 1386, 2014–2016
Luxembourg: 687, 751, 814
Malta: 1091
Moldova, Republic of: 1885
Montenegro: 1219, 1557, 1879
Netherlands: 496, 687, 690, 716, 751, 754, 814, 1418, 1566, 1618, 1795–1804, 1948
North Macedonia: 1557, 1879
Norway: 995, 1016, 1152
Poland: 814, 966, 1147, 1546, 1939, 1978, 1989, 1989, 2014–2016
Portugal: 1493–1494
Romania: 1206, 1885, 1989

Continent and Country Index

Russian Federation (west of the Urals): 957, 988, 1206, 1242, ca.1340, 1448, 1510, 1589, 1652, 1721, 1793, 1917, 1918, 1927, 1936–1938, 1958–1964, 1990
Serbia: 1219, 1557, 1879
Slovakia: 814, 1989
Slovenia: 814
Spain: 711–716, 814, 1085, 1479, 1492, 1493–1494, 1514–1517, 1572
Sweden: 829, ca.990, 1130–1155, 1895, 2014–2016
Switzerland: 687, 751, 814, 1431–1449, 1522, 1527, 1536, 1541, 1927
Ukraine: 957, 988, 1206, 1227, 1569, 1596, 1885
United Kingdom of Great Britain and Northern Ireland (England): 590, 597, 664, 731, 871–899, 1066, 1098, 1170, 1384, 1525, 1534, 1549, 1553–1558, 1559, 1563, 1604, 1641–1646, 1643–1649, 1647, 1649, 1660, 1673, 1688, 1695, 1698, 1738, 1781, 1792, 1795–1804, 1807, 1829, 1833, 1845, 1855, 1859, 1865, 1867, 1873, 1943, 1966
United Kingdom of Great Britain and Northern Ireland (Northern Ireland): 1873
United Kingdom of Great Britain and Northern Ireland (Scilly Islands): ca.990
United Kingdom of Great Britain and Northern Ireland (Scotland): 563, 995, 1560, 1596, 1843, 1873, 1910
United Kingdom of Great Britain and Northern Ireland (Wales): 1904

GRECO-ROMAN WORLD

Albania: ca.46
Algeria: 311–312, 527–565
Bosnia and Herzegovina: 527–565
Croatia: 527–565
(Cyprus): ca.46
Egypt: ca.120–160, ca.180–190, ca.190, ca.220–230, 231, ca.270, 318, 320s, 328, 367, 412
France: 177, 189, ca.190
Greco-Roman World (no further differentiation): 303–311, 311, 321, 337–361
Greece: ca.46, 50, 96, ca.130–140, 390
Italy: ca.46, ca.49, 50, 64, ca.65–ca.95, 96, ca.107, ca.120–160, 144, ca.151, 189, ca.215, 250–251, 251, 312, 330, 366–384, 386, 390, 410, 440, 452, 527–565
Libya: 527–565
Morocco: 527–565
Palestine, State of: ca.30, 49, 62, ca.65–ca.95, 66–73, 132–135, 231, 250–251, 325, 370s, 378–383
Serbia: 357
Slovenia: 527–565
Spain: ca.46, 527–565
Syrian Arab Republic: ca.65–ca.95, ca.80–100, 225
Tunisia: 180, ca.197, 203, 207, 250–251, 251, 258, 311–312, 385, 395, 418, 527–565
Turkey: ca.46, 50, ca.65–ca.95, ca.107, ca.112, ca.130–140, 156, 172, 189, Before 195, 201, 250–251, 268, 325, 330, 337, 360s–370s, 361–363, 379, 381, 387, 404, 412, 431, 449, 451

LATIN AMERICA AND THE CARIBBEAN

Argentina: 1609, 1810, 1826–1830s, 1909, 1974–1984, 2013
Bahamas: 1492
Barbados: 1712
Bolivia, Plurinational State of: 1609, 1826–1830s, 1990s

Continent and Country Index

Brazil: 1493–1494, 1500, 1549, 1555, 1609, 1652, 1824, 1872, 1889, 1891, 1896, 1964–1985
Chile: 1826–1830s, 1909, 1925, 1970
Colombia: 1826–1830s, 1955, 1966, 1968
Cuba: 1910s, 1959
Dominican Republic: 1501, 1510, 1511, 1512–1513, 1513, 1514
Ecuador: 1826–1830s, 1860–1875, 1990s
El Salvador: 1980, 1986, 1989
Guatemala: 1826–1830s, 1974–1984
Guyana: 1823
Haiti: 1501, 1510, 1511, 1512–1513, 1513, 1514
Latin America and the Caribbean (no further differentiation): 1537, 1542, 1899, 1923–1924
Mexico: 1519–1521, 1523, 1524, 1531, 1531, 1537, 1550–1551, 1552, 1555, 1570, 1810, 1826–1830s, 1857, 1867, 1910, 1929, 1979
Nicaragua: 1531, 1826–1830s, 1979–1990
Panama: 1513
Paraguay: 1587, 1609, 1641, 1826–1830s, 1974–1984, 1992
Peru: 1540, 1552, 1570, 1599, 1615, 1671, 1687, 1826–1830s, 1836–1856, 1971, 1984
Trinidad and Tobago: 1838
Uruguay: 1609, 1910s, 1961
Venezuela, Bolivarian Republic of: 1826–1830s

NORTH AMERICA

Bermuda: 1701
Canada: 1604–1605, 1608, 1625, 1639, 1649, 1701, 1763, 1948, 1994
United States of America: 1607, 1620, 1626, 1628, 1634, 1636, 1662, 1681–1682, 1692, 1701, 1734–1743, 1749, 1765–1783, 1786, 1801, 1801, 1810, 1815, 1824, 1830, 1830, 1840s, 1843–1844, 1845, 1845, 1847, 1861–1865, 1863, 1881. 1893, 1901, 1908, 1910–1915, 1914, 1915, 1917, 1925, 1928, 1947, 1949, 1955, 1960, 1960, 1967, 1968, 1969, 1979, 1987–1988, 1989, 2001

OCEANIA

American Samoa: 1830s
Australia: 1788, 1794, 1797, 1847, 2020
Cook Islands: 1821, 1823, 1839
Fiji: 1835, 1844, 1854, 1890, 1913
French Polynesia: 1769, 1796, 1815, 1817, 1819, 1834, 1844
Guam: 1668
(Hawai'i): 1820, 1824, 1837–1839
Kiribati: 1852, 1888
Marshall Islands: 1850s, 1857
Micronesia, Federated States of: 1668, 1850s, 1899–1914
New Caledonia: 1840, 1902, 1902
New Zealand: 1766, 1793, 1814, 1822, 1830, 1838, 1840, 1872, 1881, 1918, 1989
Niue: 1852
Northern Mariana Islands: 1668
Oceania (no further differentiation): 1521, 1976
Papua New Guinea: 1871, 1875, 1882, 1900, 1968, 2013
Pitcairn: 1890
Samoa: 1844, 1845, 1900, 1961
Solomon Islands: 1845, 1849, 1968
Tokelau: 1845–1863
Tonga: 1797, 1826, 1830, 1830s, 1834
Tuvalu: 1861
Vanuatu (New Hebrides): 1839, 1846
Wallis and Futuna Islands: 1836, 1837, 1841, 1842

(OUTER SPACE)

(Moon: Lunar Orbit): 1968
(Moon: Mare Tranquillitatis): 1969

Name Index

This index lists the names of those persons referred to within the timeline. Additional detail is added where necessary to distinguish between same or similar names, e.g. Adam (Ching-Ching) 781 and Adam of Bremen 948, Nicholas II (pope) 1059 and Nicholas II (tsar) 1917. Where a person is known by an alternative name, this is enclosed in brackets and is also listed in the index, e.g. Addai (Thaddeus) 104, which appears under "Thaddeus" as well as under "Addai." The numbers appended to each name refer to the year in the timeline in which that name appears (which may not coincide with the period in which the person lived). For example, the entry for Jesus Christ (ca.30, 62, 144, 268, 851, 1596, and 1687) includes his Crucifixion and Resurrection (ca.30) and also the secondary references to him in the other years cited (62, 144, 268, 851, 1596, and 1687).

Name Index

NAME AND DATE

'Abdisho 410
'Abdisho' bar Brika (Ebed-Jesu) 1318
Abdul Hamid II (sultan) 1894–1896
Abgar VIII (king) Before 195
Abraham of Kaskar 569–571
Abu 'Ali al-Ḥakim bi-'Amr-Allāh (caliph) 1009–1016
Abu Salih ca.1300
Abu'l-Faraj 987
Acacius (Mār 'Aqaq) (catholicos) 486
Adam (Ching-Ching) 781
Adam of Bremen 948
Addai (Thaddeus) 104
Adelheid (princess) 975
Adrian II (pope) 867
Adrian IV (pope) (Cardinal Nicholas Breakspear) 1152
Afonso I (Mvemba a Nzinga) (king) 1491, 1520, 1534, 1540
Afonso V ("the African") (king) 1432
Aglipay, Gregorio 1902
Ahmad ibn Ibrāhim al-Ghāzi (imām) 1531–1543
Ahn Byung Mu 1970
Ai (emperor) 907
Ai-hsueh 1289
Alcuin of York 781
Aldrin, Buzz 1969
Alexander (bishop) 318
Alexander V (pope) 1378
Alexander VI (pope) 1493–1494
Alexander VIII (pope) 1682
Alexis I (tsar) 1652
Alfonso VI (king) 1085
Alfred the Great (king) 871–899
Allende Gossens, Salvador Guillermo 1970
Alopen 635
Alvarez de Osorio, Diego 1531
Ambrose of Milan 386, 390
Amda-Simon (king) 1357
Ananias 62
Anders, Bill 1968
Andrade, Antonio de 1624
Animinanda, Brahmachari Rewachand ca.1940

Anjiro 1549
Anselm of Canterbury 1098
Anskar 829, 857
Antoine, Daniel 1649
Antoninus Pius (emperor) ca.151
Antony of Egypt ca.270
Aquinas, Thomas 1274
Aquino, Corazon 1986
Arḡūn, Il-Khan 1287
Aristeides of Athens ca.130–140
Arius 318
Arnaldur 1123
Athanasius 328, 367
Attila the Hun 452
Auala, Leonard Nangolo 1971
Augustine of Canterbury 590, 597
Augustine of Hippo 385, 386, 395
Ausoleil, Louis 1858
Azambuja, Diogo de 1482

Balboa, Vasco Nuñez de 1513
Baldeus, Philip 1658
Bar Kochba, Simon 132–135
Bar Ṣaumā 489
Barād'i, Jacob al- ca.542–578
Bardaisan 196
Barreira, Balthasar 1604
Basil of Caesarea 360s–370s, 370s
Basilides ca.120–160
Baybars (sultan) 1272
Becket, Thomas à 1170
Bede, the Venerable 731
Behaine, Pigneau de 1789
Bell, George 1943
Benedict of Aniane 779
Benedict of Nursia 529, ca.530, 779
Benedict XIV (pope) (Cardinal Prospero Lorenzo Lambertini) 1740, 1742
Benedict XV (pope) 1919
Benedict XVI (pope) 2013
Benezet, Anthony 1772
Ben-Gurion, David 1948
Benlloch y Vivó, Juan Bautista 1923–1924
Bennett, Dennis 1960
Berard of Carbio 1220

Name Index

Bergoglio, Jorge Mario (Pope Francis I) 2013, 2016
Bernard of Clairvaux 1146
Bershambo, Saif ad-Dīn ʿAbdullah (king) 1315
Berthold (bishop) 1195
Biko, Steve 1977
Bingham, Hiram 1820
Bingham, Hiram, II 1852
Björg (king) 829
Blanchet, Edward 1864
Blank, Joost de 1960
Boardman, George and Sarah 1827
Boesak, Allan 1982
Bojaxhiu, Agnes Gonxha ("Mother" Teresa) 1948, 1979, 1997, 2016
Boniface (Wynfrith) 716, 754
Boniface VIII (pope) 1302
Bonifer, Pierre 1554
Booth, William 1865
Boris I (king) 864
Borman, Frank 1968
Bort (prince) 1227
Boutros-Ghālī, Boutros 1910
Boutros-Ghālī, Pasha 1910
Bradley, Dan Beach 1835
Braide, Garrick Sokari 1912, 1916
Branham, William 1947
Bray, Thomas 1698
Breakspear, Nicholas (Pope Adrian IV) 1152
Brébeuf, Jean de 1649
Bréhéret, Jean-Baptiste 1844
Brent, Charles H. 1927
Brenz, Johannes 1563
Brown, George 1875
Bruno of Cologne 1084
Bucer, Martin 1541
Burgos, José 1872
Bush, George W. 2001
Buvanaika Bahu VII (king) 1543
Buzacott, Aaron 1839

Cabral, Pedro Álvares 1500
Caecilian 311–312
Cakobau, Seru Epenisa 1854
Callixtus II (pope) 1122

Calvert, Cecilius 1634
Calvert, James 1854
Calvin, John 1536, 1561, 1618
Camara, Hélder 1964–1985
Candidius, Georgius 1626
Canto, Sebastião da 1567
Capitein, Jacobus 1742
Carey, William 1777, 1792, 1793, 1805, 1813, 1829
Cargill, David 1835
Carlos III (king) 1768
Casolini, Annetto 1846
Castro, Fidel 1959
Catherine of Siena 1378
Celestine III (pope) 1195
Cerularius, Michael (patriarch) 1054
Cespedes, Gregorio de 1592
Champlain, Samuel de 1608
Chandra Pol, Krishna 1813
Chanel, Pierre (Peter) 1837, 1841
Charbanel, Noel 1649
Charlemagne (holy roman emperor) 751, 781, 800, 814, 962
Charles I (king) 1628, 1649
Charles II (king) 1649, 1660
Charles IX (king) 1572
Charles the Simple (king) 911
Charles V (holy roman emperor) 1521
Chastan, Jacques-Honoré 1839
Cheng Chʻeng-Kung (Koxinga) 1662
Chiang Kai-Shek 1949
Childeric (king) 751
Chilembwe, John 1913
Chiluba, Frederick 1991
Ching Tien-Ying 1922
Ching-Ching (Adam) 781
Chlodovocar (Clovis) (king) 496
Chou Wen-mo, James 1801
Chrysostom, John 404
Chulalongkorn (king) 1870
Chuma 1873
Claudius (emperor) ca.49
Clement of Alexandria ca.190
Clement of Rome 96
Clement V (pope) 1305–1377
Clement VII (pope) 1378
Clement X (pope) 1671

Name Index

Clement XI (pope) 1693
Clement XIV (pope) 1773
Clive, Robert 1757
Clovis (Chlodovocar) (king) 496
Coan, Titus 1837–1839
Codrington, Christopher 1712
Cointac, Jean de 1555
Coke, Thomas 1814
Colenso, John 1847, 1863
Colonna, Oddone (Pope Martin V) 1414–1418
Columba 563
Columbanus ca.590
Columbus, Christopher 1492
Conselheiro, Antônio 1896
Constans (emperor) 337, 361
Constantine (I) (emperor) 311, 312, 321, 325, 330, 337, 337, 361
Constantine II (emperor) 337–361
Constantine XI (emperor) 1453
Constantius II (emperor) 337–361
Contarini, Gasparo (cardinal) 1541
Cook, James, Captain 1766, 1769, 1796
Copernicus, Nicolaus 1546, 1610
Cortés, Hernán de Monroy y Pizarro Altamirano 1519–1521, 1523
Cosmas Indicopleustes 555
Covilhão, Pero da 1494
Cranmer, Thomas 1549, 1553–1558
Cromwell, Oliver 1649, 1660
Cross, William 1835
Crowther, Samuel Ajayi 1843, 1857, 1864
Cugoano, Ottobah 1787
Cyprian 251, 258
Cyriacus 1076
Cyril (bishop) 412
Cyril (missionary) 863, 867

da Gama, Vasco 1498
Dādīšo' (Dadyeshu) (catholicos) 424
Dadyeshu (Dādīšo') (catholicos) 424
Damasus 366–384
Dao Xuan (Dōsen) 735
Darwin, Charles 1859
Dawud I (king) 1272
de Klerk, Frederick Willem 1989, 1990
Decius (emperor) 250–251

Delgado, Ignatius 1821–1841
Denha (patriarch) 1275, 1281
Des Places, Claude-François Poullart 1703
Descartes, Rene 1620
Desideri, Ippolito (Hippolyte) 1716
Dhū Nuwās (king) 520
Dias, Bartolomeu 1571
Diocletian (emperor) 303–311
Diogo I (Nkumbi a Mpudi) (king) 1553
Dioscorus 449
Doane, Edward and Sarah 1857
Dōsen (Dao Xuan) 735
Duarte, José Napoleón 1986
Dupuch, Antony 1838

Eanes, Gil 1434
Ebed-Jesu ('Abdisho' bar Brika) 1318
Ebedyeshu 1009
Edward I (king) 1287
Edward VI (king) 1553–1558, 1563
Edwards, Jonathan 1734–1743
Elekana 1861
Eliot, T.S. 1170
Elizabeth I (queen) 1559
Ella Amida (king) Before 356
Engels, Friedrich 1848
Equiano, Olaudah (Gustavus Vassa) 1789
Erik IX (king) 1155
Eskender (emperor) 1494
Ethelbert (king) 597
Eugene IV (pope) 1435, 1439
Eugenius III (pope) 1146, 1147
Eusebius of Caesarea 325

Fagamanu, Mata'afa 1845
Falwell, Jerry 1979
Fasildas (emperor) 1632
Felicitas 203
Ferdinand II (king) 1479, 1492
Finlay, Robert 1822
Finney, Charles Grandison 1824, 1837–1839
Flores de Oliva, Isabel ("Saint Rose of Lima") 1671
Foucauld, Charles de 1916
Fox, George 1647

Name Index

Francis I (pope) (Cardinal Jorge Mario Bergoglio) 2013, 2016
Francis of Assisi 1210, 1219
Francisco, Jiménez de Cisneros 1514–1517
Francke, August Hermann 1694
Franklin, Benjamin 1749
Franz Ferdinand (archduke) 1914
Freeman, Thomas Birch 1838
Freitas, Jurdão de 1537
Frelinghuysen, Theodore 1734–1743
Frumentius Before 356
Fuller, Thomas 1384

Galerius (emperor) 311
Galilei, Galileo 1610
Garcia de Padilla, Francisco 1501
Garcia Moreno, Gabriel 1860–1875
Garcia Serrano, Miguel 1621
Garnier, Charles 1649
Gatu, John 1971
Geisa (Géza) (prince) 975
Genghis Khan 1206, 1241
George Tupou I (Tāufaʻāhau) (king) 1830
Georgios I (king) 836
Géza (Geisa) (prince) 975
Gia Long (Nguyễn Ánh) (emperor) 1789, 1802–1820
Ginés de Sépulveda, Juan 1550–1551
Gobat, Samuel 1830s
Goméz, Mariano 1872
González Vigil, Francisco de Paula 1836–1856
Gorbachev, Mikhail 1989, 1990
Graham, Billy 1949
Grammont, Jean-Joseph de 1783
Gray, Robert 1847, 1863
Gregory ("the Illuminator") 288
Gregory I ("the Great") (pope) 590
Gregory III (pope) 2013
Gregory IX (pope) 1232
Gregory of Nazianzus 360s–370s
Gregory of Nyssa 360s–370s
Gregory VII (pope) 1075, 1076, 1076–1077
Gregory XI (pope) 1378
Gregory XIV (pope) 1555
Gregory XV (pope) 1622
Grey, Lady Jane 1553–1558

Guáman Poma, Felipe de Ayala 1615
Gunananda Thera, Mohottivatte 1873
Gutenberg, Johannes 1450s
Gutiérrez, Gustavo 1971
Gützlaff, Karl 1844
Guzman, Dominic de 1216

Hadrian (emperor) ca.130–140
Haile Selassie (Tafari Makonnen) (emperor) 1930, 1959, 1974
Harald Bluetooth (Harald I) (king) 948
Haraldssön, Olaf (king) 1016
Hardie, Charles, 1844
Harris, Barbara 1989
Harris, James 1839
Harris, William Wade 1913, 1915, 1924
Hatta, Mohammed 1945
Hayasaka, Januarius Kyunosake 1927
Ḥayyān 356
Hearst, William Randolph 1949
Heath, Thomas 1840
Henrique, Dom 1520
Henry ("the Navigator") (prince) 1416
Henry II (king) 1170
Henry III (holy roman emperor) 1046
Henry IV (holy roman emperor) 1076–1077
Henry IV (king) 1589
Henry V (holy roman emperor) 1122
Henry VIII (king) 1534
Hidalgo y Costilla, Miguel 1810
Hippolytus of Rome ca.215
Hirth, Jean-Joseph 1900
Hong Xiuquan 1850–1864
Hoover, Herbert 1928
Hoover, Willis and Minnie 1909
Houphouët-Boigny, Félix 1990
Hoxha, Enver 1967
Huang Xing 1911
Huddleston, Trevor 1956
Hülegü, Il-Khan 1258
Humbert of Silva Candida 1054
Hus, Jan 1414
Hypatia 412

Ibn Wahb 851
Ignatius of Antioch ca.107

Name Index

Imbert, Laurent 1839
Innocent III (pope) 1198–1216, 1204
Innocent IV (pope) 1245–1247
Innocent X (pope) 1645
Irenaeus ca.190
Isaac (catholicos) 410, 410
Isabella I (queen) 1479, 1492
Isho'yabh III (catholicos) 657
Issu (Mār Yazdbozid) 781

Jacobus, Justin de 1839
James (brother of Jesus) 62
James I (king of England) = James VI (king of Scotland) 1596, 1604
James II (king) 1688
James VI (king of Scotland) = James I (king of England) 1596, 1604
Jamieson, Penny 1989
Javouhey, "Mother" 1819
Jefferson, Thomas 1786
Jeremias II (patriarch) 1589
Jerome 378–383
Jesus Christ ca.30, 62, 144, 268, 851, 1596, 1687
Jesus, Venossa de 1835
Jiaqing (emperor) 1800
Joanna I (queen) 1512–1513
João I (Nzinga a Nkuwu) (king) 1491
João III (king) 1543, 1549
John of Leyden 1534–1535
John of Plano Carpini 1245–1247, 1265–1266
John Paul II (pope) (Cardinal Karol Wojtyla) 1978, 1979, 1984, 1984, 1989, 1990, 1997
John XI (patriarch) 1439
John XXIII (pope) (Cardinal Angelo Giuseppe Roncalli) 1958
Jonas (metropolitan) 1448
Jones, E. Stanley 1920s
Jones, John Taylor 1893
Juárez Garcia, Benito Pablo 1857, 1867
Judson, Adoniram 1813, 1817, 1824–1826, 1826, 1827, 1835
Judson, Ann Hasseltine 1817
Julian (monk) 543

Julian the Apostate (emperor) 340–363, 361–363
Julius II (pope) 1506
Justin Martyr ca.151
Justinian (emperor) 527–565, 551

Ka'ahumanu (queen regent) 1824
Kagawa Toyohiko 1940
Kaleb (king) 520
Kam, Joseph Carel 1815
Kanoa, J. W. 1852
Kao-Tsung (emperor) 698
Kasa (Tewodros (Theodore)) (emperor) 1855
Kaunda, Kenneth 1960, 1964, 1991
Kavad (king) 497–498
Ked-Buka 1258
Kempis, Thomas à 1418
Kennedy, John F. 1960
Kgama III (kgosi) ca.1860
Khrushchev, Nikita 1958–1964
Kierkegaard, Søren 1843
Kim Chin-Ki 1876
Kim Sou-hwan, Stephen (cardinal) 1969
Kim Tae-Kon, Andrew 1846
Kimbangu, Simon 1915, 1918, 1921, 1959
Kimpa Vita, Dona Beatriz 1665
Kināyi, Thomas 345
King, Martin Luther, Jr. 1968
Kiwánuka, Joseph 1939
Klak, Harald (king) 829
Knox, John, 1560
Knut (king) 1022, 1026
Ko Thah A 1826
Ko Thah Byu 1827
Koeberle, Joseph 1864
Kong Hee 1989, 2010
Koxinga (Cheng Ch'eng-Kung) 1662
Krapf, Johann Ludwig 1842, 1844
Kublai Khan 1245–1247, 1265–1266, 1289

L'Incarnation, Marie de 1639
La Cruz, Jeronimo de 1567
Lalemant, Gabriel 1649
Lambert de la Motte, Pierre 1664
Lambertini, Prospero Lorenzo (Pope Benedict XIV) 1740, 1742

Name Index

Laoghaire (Lóegaire) mac Néill (king) 432
Las Casas, Bartolomé de 1514, 1550–1551, 1552
Latimer, Hugh 1553–1558
Laval, Jacques-Desire 1841–1842
Lavelua (king) 1836
Lavigerie, Charles 1868
Lawry, Walter 1826
Le Roux, Petrus Louis 1903
Le Vavasseur, Frédéric 1841–1842
Lee (Yi) Seung-Hun 1783, 1789–1790, 1801
Lee (Yi) Song-Ha 1876
Lee (Yi) Ung-Ch'an 1876
Leenhardt, Maurice 1902
Leigh, Samuel and Catherine 1822
Lenin (Vladimir Ilyich Ulyanov) 1917
Lenshina, Alice 1953, 1955, 1964
Leo I (pope) 440, 452
Leo IX (pope) 1049
Leo XIII (pope) 1891
Leopold II (king) 1885
Leria, Jean de 1642
Lespinasse Saune, Henri de 1925
Liang Fa 1816
Libermann, François-Marie-Paul 1841–1842
Lichtenburg, Bernhard 1938
Licinius (emperor) 312
Lievans, Constant 1885
Lincoln, Abraham 1863
Livingstone, David 1847, 1853–1856, 1856, 1857, 1858, 1871, 1873
Llull, Ramon 1293
Locke, John 1695
Lóegaire mac Néill (Laoghaire) (king) 432
Lombard, Peter ca.1157
Lon Nol 1990
Longley, Charles Thomas 1867
López de Legazpi, Miguel 1565
López, Gregory (Luo Wenzao) 1656
Louis Phillipe (king) 1819
Louis the Pious (holy roman emperor) 814
Louis VII (king) 1146
Louis XIV (king) 1598, 1685
Lovell, James 1968
Loyola, Ignatius 1540

Lugard, Fredrick 1890
Luis de Sanvitores, Diego 1668
Luo Wenzao (Gregory López) 1656
Luther, Martin 1517, 1521
Lyman, Henry 1833

Mabuza, Meshack 2012
Mackintosh, Aeneas 1916
Magalhães, Fernão de (Ferdinand Magellan) 1521
Magellan, Ferdinand (Fernão de Magalhães) 1521
Magnus (bishop) 1291
Maharasan, Vedamanikam 1818
Mahdī (caliph) 781
Maigrot, Charles (bishop) 1693
Makhanda, Nxele 1811
Makonnen, Tafari (Haile Selassie) (emperor) 1930, 1959, 1974
Malaspina, Alejandro 1793
Malek al-Kāmel Nāṣer-al-dīn al- (sultan) 1219
Mandela, Nelson 1990, 1994
Mao Zedong 1949, 1966–1976
Mār Abā (catholicos) 540
Mār 'Aqaq (Acacius) (catholicos) 486
Mār Bābay 569–571
Mār Sargis 578
Mār Yazdbozid (Issu) 781
Marcion 144
Marcos, Ferdinand 1972, 1986
Maria de Genova, Carlo 1710–1711
Marignolli, Giovanni de 1346
Marin, Esteban 1601
Mark (Yaballaha III) (patriarch) 1275, 1281, 1318
Marsden, Samuel 1794, 1797, 1814
Marshman, Joshua 1805
Martel, Charles 732, 751
Martin V (pope) (Oddone Colonna) 1414–1418
Martyn, Henry 1806
Marx, Karl 1848
Mason, Francis 1857
Massaja, Guglielmo 1839
Maubant, Pierre-Philibert 1839
Maung Naw 1813

Name Index

Māwiyya (queen) 373
Maximilian I (emperor) 1867
Maximilla 172
Medici, Catherine de' 1572
Melancthon, Philip 1541
Melville, Andrew 1596
Menelik II (king) 1896
Menezes, Alexis de 1599
Mengistu Haile Mariam 1991
Menster, William 1947
Měšīḥā-Zěḵā 225
Methodius 863, 867
Mieszko I (prince) 966
Milingo, Emmanuel 1983
Miller, William 1843–1844
Milne, William 1816
Mindowe (king) ca.1251
Minh Mạng (emperor) 1821–1841
Mobutu, Joseph-Désiré 1965, 1972
Moffat, Robert 1817
Mokone, Mangena Maake 1892
Mongkut (Rama IV) (king) 1851
Montanus 172
Montesinos, Antonio de 1511
Moody, Dwight L. 1873
Morrison, Robert 1807, 1816
Moses 851
Moshoeshoe 1833
"Mother" Teresa (Agnes Gonxha Bojaxhiu) 1948, 1979, 1997, 2016
Muḥammad (prophet) 610, 622
Muḥammad Ahmad, bin Abd Allah (mahdī) 1898
Muḥammad II (sultan) 1453
Munson, Samuel 1833
Müntzer, Thomas 1524–1525
Mussolini, Benito 1929, 1935
Mutesa I, Walugembe Mukaabya (king) 1874
Muzorewa, Abel Tendekayi 1978
Mvemba a Nzinga (Afonso I) (king) 1491, 1520, 1534, 1540
Mwanga II (king) 1886, 1890

Nan Inta 1875
Nana (queen) ca.330
Nāsser, Ǧamāl Abdel 1956

Nee, Watchman (Ni To-sheng) 1926
Nero (emperor) 64
Nestorius 412, 431
Nevius, John L. 1890
Nevsky, Alexander 1242
Newman, John Henry 1845
Nguéma, Francisco Macias 1968
Nguyễn Ánh (Gia Long) (emperor) 1789, 1802–1820
Nguyễn Bá Tòng, Jean Baptiste 1933
Ni To-sheng (Watchman Nee) 1926
Nicholas II (pope) 1059
Nicholas II (tsar) 1917
Nikon (patriarch) 1652
Nimeiri, Jaafar al- 1955
Nino ca.330
Niuliki (king) 1841
Nixon, Richard 1860
Nkrumah, Kwame 1957, 1960
Nkumbi a Mpudi (Diogo I) (king) 1553
Noah 851
Nobili, Robert de 1605
Nóbrega, Manuel da 1549
Nommensen, Ludwig 1862
Ntsikana 1811
Nyerere, Julius 1960
Nzinga a Nkuwu (João I) (king) 1491

O'Hair, Madalyn Murray 1969
O'Sullivan, John 1845
Odinkar Hvite (the elder) ca.990
Olaf the White 851
Olga (grand princess) 957
Oppong, Sampson 1920
Origen ca.220–230, 231
Oswy, 664
Otto I (holy roman emperor) 955, 962
Otto of Freising 1145

Pachomius, 320s
Paez, Pedro 1622
Page, Albert and Lou 1913
Paik Hong-Chun 1876
Pantaenus ca.180–190, ca.190
Papeiha 1821
Parham, Charles Fox 1901
Park, Rosa 1955

Name Index

Parker, Matthew 1563
Parker, Peter 1834
Patrick 432
Paul (apostle) ca.46, 50, 144, 1091
Paul III (pope) 1537, 1540
Paul of Samosata 268
Paul VI (pope) 1966, 1968, 1969, 1976
Paulo 1852
Pedro II (emperor) 1872, 1889
Pegado, Vicente 1531
Pell, George (cardinal) 2020
Penn, William 1681–1682
Pepin III (king) 751
Pepin of Heristal (king) 687, 751
Perkins, Justin 1834
Perpetua 203
Perraux, Fr. 1876
Peter (apostle) 366–384
Peter the Great (tsar) 1721
Petitjean, Bernard 1865
Philip III (king) 1615
Philip, John 1820, 1834–1835
Pierson, George and Nancy 1854
Pilkington, George 1893
Pinochet, Augusto 1970
Pitt, William (the younger) 1784
Pius IX (pope) 1854, 1868
Pius XI (pope) 1919, 1927, 1929, 1933
Pius XII (pope) 1854, 1950
Pkidha (bishop) 104
Pliny (the younger) ca.112
Plutschau, Heinrich 1706
Pol Pot 1990
Polo, Maffeo 1265–1266, 1275
Polo, Marco 1265–1266, 1275
Polo, Niccolò 1265–1266, 1275
Polycarp (bishop) 156
Pōmare II (king) 1819
Pompallier, Jean Baptiste 1838
Porres, Martin de 1599
Portes Gil, Emilio Cándido 1929
Pratt, Addison 1844
Prester John (king) 1145, 1494, 1515
Price, Jonathan 1824–1826
Princip, Gavrilan 1914
Prisca 172
Prodhomme, Fr. 1876

Quadratus ca.130–140
Quaque, Philip 1765
Quiroga, Vasco de 1537

Radama I (king) 1820, 1835, 1861
Radama II (king) 1861, 1868
Raffles, Sir Stamford 1819
Raikes, Robert 1781
Rama IV (Mongkut) (king) 1851
Ramabai, Pandita 1909
Ramarosandratna, Ignace 1925
Ramsey, Michael 1966
Ranavalona I (queen) 1835–1861
Ranavalona II (queen) 1868
Rātana, Tahupōtiki Wiremu 1918, 1918
Ratislav (prince) 863
Rauschenbusch, Walter 1917
Ray, James Earl 1968
Read, James 1829
Rhodes, Alexandre de 1624
Ricci, Matteo 1582, 1600, 1603, 1603
Richards, Henry 1886
Ridley, Nicholas 1553–1558
Riis, Andreas 1828
Rimitsu 735
Rio Branco, baron of (José Maria da Silva Paranhos) 1872
Roberts, Evan 1904
Roberts, Oral 1947
Roger I (king) 1091
Rollo 911
Romero y Galdámez, Óscar Arnulfo 1980
Roncalli, Angelo Giuseppe (Pope John XXIII) 1958
Rose of Lima, Saint (Isabel Flores de Oliva) 1671
Roulleaux, Joseph-François 1844
Rudahigwa, Mutara III (king) 1946
Rugambwa, Laurean 1960
Russell, Charles Taze 1881
Ruyl, Albert Cornelius 1629

Sādāt, Anwār al- 1981
Saladin (Ṣalāḥ-al-dīn Yūsof ibn Ayyūb) 1187
Ṣalāḥ-al-dīn Yūsof ibn Ayyūb (Saladin) 1187

Name Index

Salazar, Domingo de 1571
Salvado, Rosendo 1847
Sankey, Ira D. 1873
Šāpur II (king) 340–363
Saturninus 180
Ṣaumā 1275, 1287
Sava, Saint 1219
Savanarola, Girolamo 1498
Saw Quala 1857
Schleiermacher, Friedrich 1799
Schmelen, Heinrich 1811
Schmidt, Georg 1738, 1792
Schütz, Roger 1940
Schwartz, Christian Friedrich 1750
Schweitzer, Albert 1913
Scopes, John 1925
Sechele I (kgosi) 1847
Segundo, Juan Luis 1961
Senghor, Leopold 1960
Seraphim of Sarov 1793
Sergii of Radonezh ca.1340
Serra, Joseph 1847
Shackleton, Sir Ernest 1916
Shaka 1816
Shem'on (metropolitan) 657
Shembe, Isaiah 1910
Shenouda III (patriarch) 1981
Shinsui, Kawai 1927
Shrewsbury, William 1834–1835
Silesia, Severino da 1710–1711
Silva de Mendouça, Lourenço da 1686
Silva Paranhos, José Maria da (baron of Rio Branco) 1872
Silva, David Wickrametilleke de 1873
Sin, Jaime Lachica (cardinal) 1976
Sjarifuddin, Amir 1945
Slessor, Mary 1846
Smith, Alfred E. 1928
Smith, John 1823
Smith, Joseph 1830, 1844, 1847
Sobrino, Jon 1989
Sorqaqtani-Beki (princess) 1252
Spener, Philipp Jakob 1675, 1694
Stanley, Sir Henry Morton 1871, 1874
Stragorodskii, Sergii (metropolitan) 1927
Strategopoulos, Alexios Komnenos 1261
Suh Sang-Yun 1883

Sukarno, Ahmad 1945
Suleiman the Magnificent (emperor) 1526–1529, 1557
Sumuafa' Ashawa' 520
Sun Yat-Sen 1911
Suriyawong, Somdet Chao Phraya Si 1870
Susi 1873
Susneyos (emperor) 1622, 1632
Sverker (king) 1130–1155

Tabarija (king) 1537
Tabuyo, Augustin 1621
Tai-Tsung (emperor) 638
Tamerlane (emperor) By 1370
Tatian ca.170
Tāufa'āhau (George Tupou I) (king) 1830
Tay, John I. 1890
Taylor, Hudson, 1865
Te Kooti, Arikirangi Te Turuki 1872
Te Toiroa, Arama 1766
Te Whiti-o-Rongomai, III, Erueti 1881
Templier, Guillaume 1901
Tennent, Gilbert 1734–1743
Teresa of Ávila 1572
Teresa, "Mother" (Agnes Gonxha Bojaxhiu) 1948, 1979, 1997, 2016
Tertullian ca.197, 207
Tewodros (Theodore) (Kasa) (emperor) 1855
Tewophilos (patriarch, abuna) 1974
Thaddeus (Addai) 104
Theodora, Empress 543
Theodosius I (emperor) 379, 387, 390
Theophilus 739
Theophilus the Deacon 356
Thévenoud, Johanny 1921
Thomas (apostle) 52
Thomas, John 1826, 1830
Thomas, Robert Jermain 1865
Thompson, Thomas 1752, 1765
Thorkilsen, Asser 1123
Tile, Nehemiah 1883
Timotheos I (catholicos) 779, 781
Timothy II (patriarch) 1318
Tiridates III (king) 288
Tisserant, Eugene 1841–1842
Toghrul, Wang-Khan (king) 1145

Name Index

Tokugawa Hidetada 1622
Tokugawa Ieyasu 1600, 1601, 1614, 1616
Toland, John 1696
Torres Restrepo, Camilo 1966
Toynbee, Arnold 1915–1918
Toyotomi Hideyoshi 1587, 1598
Trajan (emperor) ca.112
Triaire, Fr. 1858
Tribhuwanottunggadewī Jayawiṣṇu-wardhanī (queen regent) 1346
Tryggvessön, Olaf (king) ca.990, 995, 1004, 1016
Tudor, Mary ("Bloody Mary") (queen) 1553–1558
Tupas, Raja 1565
Turner, George 1844
Tutu, Desmond 1984, 1986
Tyndale, William 1525

Ulfilas 341
Ulyanov, Vladimir Ilyich (Lenin) 1917
'Umar I (caliph) 638
Urban II (pope) 1085, 1095
Urban VI (pope) 1378
Urdaneta, Andrés de 1565

Vahapata 1821
Valentinus ca.120–160
Valerian (emperor) 258
Valguarnera, Thomas 1655–1709
Valignano, Alessandro 1579, 1582
Van der Kemp, Johannes 1799, 1810
Varthema, Girolamo de 1510
Vassa, Gustavus (Olaudah Equiano) 1789
Veloso, Gonzalo 1534
Venn, Henry 1855
Verwoerd, Hendrik 1950
Vey, Jean-Louis 1876
Victoria (queen) 1829
Vieira, Antonio 1652
Villegaignon, Nicolas Durand de 1555
Virgin Mary, the 1854, 1879 on, 1950, 1968
Vladimir (grand prince) 988
Vogt, François Xavier 1922–1943
Von Zinzendorf, Nicholas 1722
Vorster, John 1971

Waddell, Hope M. 1846
Wamukoya, Ellinah Ntombi 2012
Wang P'an 1582
Ward, William 1805
Wesley, John 1738
Weston, Frank 1908, 1913
White, William 1822
Whitefield, George, 1734–1743
Wilberforce, William 1807
William I (king) 1820
William of Orange (prince) 1688
William of Rubruck 1265–1266
William the Conqueror (king) 1066
Williams, John 1817, 1821, 1823, 1830s, 1839
Williams, Roger 1636
Willibrord 690
Wingfield, Edward Maria 1607
Winslow, Jack 1922
Wojtyla, Karol (Pope John Paul II) 1978, 1979, 1984, 1984, 1989, 1990, 1997
Wu Hou, Empress 698
Wu Yao-tsung (Y. T. Wu) 1951
Wu-tsung (emperor) 840–846
Wycliffe, John 1384
Wynfrith (Boniface) 716, 754

Xavier, Francis 1542, 1545, 1546–1547, 1549, 1552
Xu Guangshi 1603
Xuan-tsung (emperor) 851

Yaballaha III (Mark) (patriarch) 1275, 1281, 1318
Yano Mototaka (Yano Ryūsan) 1865
Yano Ryūsan (Yano Mototaka) 1865
Yazdegerd I (shah) 410
Yi (Lee) Seung-Hun 1783, 1789–1790, 1801
Yi (Lee) Song-Ha 1876
Yi (Lee) Ung-Ch'an 1876
Yohannes IV (emperor) 1878
Young, Brigham 1847
Yung Cheng (emperor) 1724

Zakaryas (shaikh) 1892
Zamora, Jacinto 1872
Zapata, Emiliano 1910

Name Index

Zara' Ya'eqob (emperor) 1436
Ziegenbalg, Bartholomaeus 1706
Zumárraga, Juan de 1531
Zurenuoc, Theodore 2013
Zwingli, Huldrych 1522

Selected Resources

Badr, Ḥabīb, et al., eds. *Christianity: A History in the Middle East*. Beirut, Lebanon: Middle East Council of Churches, 2005.

Bowers, Paul. "Nubian Christianity: The Neglected Heritage." *African Journal of Evangelical Theology* 4.1 (1985) 3–23.

Cleary, Edward J. "The Transformation of Latin American Christianity, c.1950–2000." In *Cambridge History of Christianity*, edited by Hugh McLeod, 9:366–84. Cambridge: Cambridge University Press, 2006.

Davidson, Ivor. *The Birth of the Church: From Jesus to Constantine, AD30–312*. Monarch History of the Church 1, edited by John D. Woodbridge et al. Oxford: Monarch, 2005.

———. *A Public Faith: From Constantine to the Medieval World, AD312–600*. Monarch History of the Church 2, edited by John D. Woodbridge et al. Oxford: Monarch, 2005.

England, John C. *The Hidden History of Christianity in Asia: The Churches of the East Before 1500*. Delhi: ISPCK, 1998.

Ernst, Manfred. *Winds of Change: Rapidly Growing Religious Groups in the Pacific Islands*. Suva: Pacific Conference of Churches, 1994.

Ernst, Manfred, and Anna Anisi. "The Historical Development of Christianity in Oceania." In *The Wiley Blackwell Companion to World Christianity*, 1st ed., edited by Lamin Sanneh and Michael J. McClymond, 588–604. Chichester: Wiley-Blackwell, 2016.

Garrett, John. *To Live Among the Stars: Christian Origins in Oceania*. Geneva: World Council of Churches, in association with the Institute of Pacific Studies, University of the South Pacific, 1985.

Gillman, Ian, and Hans-Joachim Klimkeit. *Christians in Asia before 1500*. Richmond, Surrey: Curzon, 1999.

Hill, Jonathan, ed. *Zondervan Handbook to the History of Christianity*. Oxford: Lion, 2006.

Hollister, C. Warren. *Medieval Europe: A Short History*. 7th ed. New York: McGraw-Hill, 1994.

Isichei, Elizabeth. *A History of Christianity in Africa: From Antiquity to the Present*. London: SPCK, 1995.

Jenkins, Philip. *The Lost History of Christianity: The Thousand-Year Golden Age of the Church in the Middle East, Africa, and Asia—and How It Died*. New York: HarperOne, 2008.

Selected Resources

———. *The Next Christendom: The Coming of Global Christianity.* 3rd ed. Oxford: Oxford University Press, 2011.

Johnson, Todd M. "Christianity in Global Context: Trends and Statistics." Pew Forum on Religion and Public Life. http://www.pewforum.org/files/2005/05/051805-global-christianity.pdf.

Knowles, Brett. "Timeline." In *Encyclopedia of Christianity in the Global South*, edited by Mark A. Lamport, 2:959–82. Blue Ridge Summit, PA: Rowman and Littlefield, 2018.

———. "'To China with Love?' A Critical Examination of the Factors which Facilitated the Spread of Christianity in Asia up to 1000CE." In *Proceedings of the Research Group for Asian and Pacific Christianity and Cultures 1993–1994*, edited by Brett Knowles, 23–57. Dunedin: Faculty of Theology, University of Otago, 1995.

Korschorke, Klaus, et al., eds. *A History of Christianity in Asia, Africa, and Latin America, 1450–1990: A Documentary Sourcebook.* Grand Rapids: Eerdmans, 2007.

Marty, Martin. *The Christian World: A Global History.* New York: Modern Library, 2009.

McManners, John, ed. *The Oxford Illustrated History of Christianity.* Oxford: Oxford University Press, 1995.

Moffett, Samuel Hugh. *A History of Christianity in Asia. Volume I: Beginnings to 1500.* San Francisco: Harpers 1992.

———. *A History of Christianity in Asia. Volume II: 1500–1900.* American Society of Missiology Series 36. Maryknoll, NY: Orbis, 2005.

Neill, Stephen. *A History of Christian Missions.* Pelican History of the Church 6. 2nd ed., edited by Owen Chadwick. Harmondsworth: Penguin, 1986.

Quasten, Johannes. *Patrology.* 4 vols. Westminster, ML: Christian Classics, 1983.

Roberts, J.M. *The Penguin History of the World.* Rev. ed. Harmondsworth: Penguin, 1995.

Ross, Emma George. "African Christianity in Ethiopia." In *Heilbrunn Timeline of Art History.* New York: Metropolitan Museum of Art, 2000–.http://www.metmuseum.org/toah/hd/acet/hd_acet.htm (October 2002).

Salinas, J. Daniel. "The In-Roads of Evangelical Theology and the Evangelical Movement in Latin American Spanish-Speaking Countries." *Evangelical Review of Theology* 34:4 (2010) 307–12.

Sīrāfī, Abū Zayd al-. "Akhbār al-Ṣīn wʾal-Hind." In *Two Arabic Travel Books: Accounts of India and China. Abū Zayd al-Sīrāfī*, edited and translated by Tim Mackintosh-Smith, 4–161. Library of Arabic Literature. New York: New York University Press, 2014.

Soekmono, R. *Pengantar Sejarah Kebudayaan Indonesia [Introduction to Indonesian Cultural History]* 2. Yogyakarta: Penerbit Kanisius, 1973.

Stevenson, J., ed. *Creeds, Councils and Controversies: Documents illustrating the history of the Church to AD337-461.* Rev. ed., revised by W. H. C. Frend. London: SPCK, 1991.

———. ed. *A New Eusebius: Documents illustrating the history of the Church to AD337.* Rev. ed., revised by W.H.C. Frend. London: SPCK, 1992.

Sundkler, Bengt and Christopher Steed, *A History of the Church in Africa.* Cambridge: Cambridge University Press, 2000.

Sunquist, Scott W., ed. *A Dictionary of Asian Christianity.* Grand Rapids, MI: Eerdmans, 2001.

Tilley, Maureen A. "The Collapse of a Collegial Church: North African Christianity on the Eve of Islam." *Theological Studies* 62 (2001) 3–22.

United Nations Statistics Division. "Methodology: Standard country or area codes for statistical use (M49): Geographic Regions." http://unstats.un.org/unsd/methodology/m49/.

www.ingramcontent.com/pod-product-compliance
Lightning Source LLC
Chambersburg PA
CBHW060821190426
43197CB00038B/2180